MIKE GARBER

From Busy to Better

Redefining Productivity for the Modern Commercial Team

First edition

ISBN: 979-8-218-70043-0

This book was professionally typeset on Reedsy.
Find out more at reedsy.com

Dedicated to my wife (Karen) and my kids (Liam, Camila, Marie).

Thank you to my family, mentors, friends, and colleagues. Everyone I have worked with closely during my journey in education, enablement, and productivity.

Thank you to everyone who bounced ideas and provided feedback.

And a few more by name: LWP, Stacey, Frank, Chris, Lynn.

With honor to my Heavenly Father, my Savior, and the Holy Spirit.

Contents

Foreword

I've had productivity on the brain since 2018. Back then I couldn't quite name what it was I was wrestling with, but I knew something was "off." A mentor of mine helped me realize that everyone seemed to define productivity differently. For some, it was output. For others, it was streamlining. For me, I needed to figure that out.

Looking back, it had always been a driving force in my life. In my time in retail banking, in graduate school, in the way I led teams. I thought that I was chasing "operational excellence" because I was looking for better ways for people to do meaningful work that mattered.

When I started down the path of enablement, I saw it in retail, devices, SaaS, and service organizations. Commercial teams were full of good people stuck in bad systems. Output was celebrated over outcomes. Burnout was disguised as busyness. I started to see that too many people were operating with a productivity playbook that I feel was deeply outdated.

That's what this book challenges.

I propose a new way to think about productivity.

A way that doesn't focus on doing more for the sake of doing more. But on that focuses on aligning people, processes, and technology to achieve the outcomes that matter most. I focus on the commercial team because they are often the frontline for busyness burnout and outdated systems.

This is not a manifesto on hustle, or even a guide to occupational minimalism. It is a practical, grounded, and sometimes hard look at what it really takes to help move your teams from busy to better.

Yes, you'll find frameworks, examples, and principles. But most importantly, you will find permission to rethink the systems you've inherited and instead build ones that work for you.

Introduction

Productivity used to mean progress, but now it seems to mean exhaustion.

If you lead or work in a modern commercial team, you already know there's a problem. Your team is always on, with an ever-growing to-do list and constant checking of dashboards, yet somehow the business is still stuck. Every quarter demands more while also requiring you to shift your focus to another fire that the board just decided is a priority. And every tool that was supposed to help... just adds to the noise.

The real problem is deeper than most realize. You're using an old map in a new landscape.

We've inherited a model of productivity designed for a different era where output equaled success. Make more widgets, do more tasks, send more emails, log more calls. Volume was the game, and motion looked like progress. That model made sense when work was linear, repeatable, and physical. But it doesn't hold up in modern commercial teams, where outcomes are driven by strategy, clarity, creativity, and trust.

But still, most organizations continue to cling to it. They track the wrong things. Reward the wrong behavior. Burn out good people. Then panic when results don't follow.

And that's the trap. We're managing activity, not impact. We're optimizing motion, not progress. We're overworking teams without building the capacity they need to succeed. This book is your way out.

From Busy to Better is a catalyst for redefining productivity in the context of commercial work. It's for leaders and teams who want to build performance systems that scale without sacrificing culture, clarity, or their own sanity.

It's not about squeezing more out of already-overloaded teams. It's about building capacity: the ability to focus on what matters, execute with precision, and adapt without burning out.

We'll walk through how to:

- Replace outdated output metrics with outcome-based measurement.
- Streamline teams and systems without gutting your culture.
- Use AI and automation to expand human potential.
- Select and implement tools that reduce drag instead of adding noise.
- Lead change thoughtfully, with reinforcement and clarity.

This book combines frameworks, stories, and gut-check questions grounded on years of experience.

Who This Is For

First, let me define what I mean by modern commercial team. These are who are responsible for generating revenue and driving business growth, and those who support them, and may also be called a Customer-Facing Team (CFT). While each organization can define their teams as they see fit, the most common members of the commercial team include Sales, Customer Success (CS), Marketing, Enablement, Partner Management & Success, Commercial Strategy (Strategy), Consulting Services, or Operations (Ops). If your team isn't directly named, don't worry- you can still use the information found in this book for your role.

If you lead a Software-As-A-Service (SaaS) commercial or Go-To-Market (GTM) team and find yourself constantly asking: "Why are we doing all this work and still not moving the needle?" This is for you.

If you're an enablement or revenue leader trying to build systems that scale...

If you're a frontline manager trying to shield your team from burnout while still hitting the number...

If you're a Customer Success Manager (CSM), Business Development Representative (BDR), or Account Executive (AE) wondering why more work isn't leading to better results...

This book will help you name the patterns, shift the mindset, and reset the system.

You don't need to grind harder.

You need to build better systems that let good people do great work. But that starts with a new definition of productivity built on clarity, capacity, and outcomes.

We need to stop viewing busyness as a badge of honor and call it out for what it is, a red flag. Instead, we need to do more of what matters, and make it repeatable, scalable, and sustainable.

1

The Productivity Dilemma

Most teams today are overwhelmed, overworked, and under-performing. They aren't lazy, they're just using the wrong map. The old productivity playbook doesn't fit the modern world. It's time to redefine success as more meaningful achievement.

> "Nothing is less productive than to make more efficient what should not be done at all."
> —Peter Drucker

People have long viewed productivity primarily through the lens of output. How many berries did you pick? How many animals did you catch? How much corn did you grow?

Through the industrial revolution, we stayed focused on output. And this makes sense as we automated and revolutionized how to create and build. How many widgets did you make? This was important because the number of widgets directly correlated to the number of finished products, which was how much you could sell. The output drove the outcome.

However, even though the digital revolution, and now the beginnings of an AI revolution, we have still been largely focused on output. While this makes sense in manufacturing and other output-driven industries, in software and SaaS industries, the outcome is far more important than output.

Even today, most leaders and companies consider the amount of activity you do as the yardstick by which they measure your value. Of course, each of us creates output through activity. Some of one team's output is needed before another can start their activities: an assembly-line needs the widget before building the item, a marketing team needs specs and features from the production team before creating messaging and campaigns. But the true measure of productivity should not be the number of calls made, the number of emails sent, the number of slides prepared or perhaps even the number of hours worked. It should be measured by what moves the business forward.

Allow me to take a moment and define what I view as the "modern commercial team". My target audience is SaaS, Software, and Services companies, but other sectors can undoubtedly benefit. These teams are focused on driving revenue by either creating content that directly affects the customer or interacting directly with the customer. Think Marketing, Business Development, Sales, Customer Success, Consulting, Partner Management, and those who support them, like Enablement, Strategy, and Operations. In my experience, combining Enablement, Strategy and Operations into a Commercial Productivity team has streamlined roles and clarified needs many times.

In these commercial teams, traditional framing no longer applies. High output without the associated high outcome is a silent killer of modern organizations.

The gap between motion and progress is at the heart of what I call the productivity dilemma.

Historical Perspectives on Productivity

Early productivity measures were largely labor-centric, focusing on the efficiency of manual processes. The Industrial Revolution marked a significant turning point, as mechanization allowed for mass production and a dramatic increase in output. This period highlighted the importance of optimizing labor with machines, leading to the development of assembly line techniques that revolutionized manufacturing. Managers began to understand that productivity was not solely about individual worker output, but also about how systems and processes could be designed to enhance efficiency.

In the early 20th century, the introduction of scientific management principles by Frederick Taylor further refined productivity concepts. Taylor emphasized time-motion studies and standardized work processes, aiming to identify the most efficient ways to perform tasks. His approach laid the groundwork for modern management practices and encouraged a focus on maximizing output through systematic analysis. This era also saw the rise of human resource management as a critical part of productivity: managers started to recognize the value of worker satisfaction and engagement in achieving higher productivity levels.

The mid-20th century brought about significant changes with the advent of information technology. The introduction of computers and automated systems fundamentally altered workplace dynamics, enabling organizations to collect and analyze vast amounts of data. This revolution allowed for more informed decision-making and strategic planning, leading to enhanced capacity management and resource allocation. Companies began to embrace automation not just as a means of increasing production but as a way to streamline operations and improve overall productivity. The focus shifted from mere labor output to a holistic view of organizational efficiency.

To understand why we need a new productivity model, it's worth briefly revisiting how we got here. Productivity has always evolved with the nature of work — and now, in SaaS and services, we've entered a new era. Moving into the late 20th and early 21st centuries, the concept of productivity expanded to include knowledge work and the impact of globalization. The rise of the internet transformed the workplace, enabling remote work and collaboration across borders. This period emphasized the importance of agility and adaptability in productivity strategies, as organizations needed to respond to transforming market conditions. Capacity planning became essential for effective resource management and operational scalability. Now we can respond to demand fluctuations without sacrificing quality or performance.

Today, people increasingly view productivity through the lens of automation and digital transformation. Organizations are using artificial intelligence and advanced analytics to refine processes and enhance decision-making capabilities. This shift underscores the need for managers and teams to embrace new technologies as integral tools for improving productivity. Capacity planning has also evolved, requiring leaders to consider not only current resource needs but also future trends and potential disruptions. Understanding historical perspectives on productivity allows today's leaders to make informed decisions that align technology, human resources, and strategic goals, ultimately creating a more productive and resilient workplace.

The Traditional Efficiency Model: Doing More with Less

The traditional efficiency model, often encapsulated by the mantra of "doing more with less," has long been a cornerstone of productivity strategies in various sectors. This model emphasizes the optimization of resources—be it time, personnel, or materials—to maximize output while minimizing waste. For managers and commercial teams, understanding this model is crucial, as it lays the groundwork for effective capacity planning and resource management. By using established practices, organizations can streamline operations and create a more agile workforce capable of responding to shifting market demands.

At the heart of the traditional efficiency model is the concept of continuous improvement. Techniques such as Lean and Six Sigma have been widely adopted to eliminate inefficiencies and enhance productivity. These methodologies encourage teams to analyze workflows and identify bottlenecks, allowing managers to implement targeted strategies that improve throughput. For revenue teams, this means not only increasing sales but also refining processes that lead to higher conversion rates and better customer satisfaction. By fostering a culture of ongoing evaluation and adjustment, organizations can ensure that they are not just meeting, but exceeding performance benchmarks.

Another critical aspect of the traditional efficiency model is the strategic allocation of resources. Effective capacity planning involves understanding current capabilities and forecasting future needs based on market trends and business goals. Managers must assess their team's skills, technological capabilities, and tools to align resources with organizational goals. This proactive approach enables companies to predict challenges and seize opportunities, ensuring that they stay competitive in an ever-developing landscape. As automation technologies continue to advance, the ability to plan capacity effectively becomes even more vital.

Automation plays a transformative role in enhancing the traditional efficiency model. By integrating automation into workplace processes, organizations can reduce manual tasks, minimize errors, and free up employees to focus on higher-value activities. For instance, automating routine administrative tasks allows sales teams to spend more time engaging with clients and developing strategic relationships. This shift not only improves productivity but also contributes to employee satisfaction, as workers can concentrate on work that is more meaningful and impactful.

The factory-like measurements work when tasks are repeatable and logistics rarely change. However, SaaS and knowledge industries are different. Creativity, relationship-building, emotional intelligence, champion-building, and grit are not easily calculated on a dashboard. The mistake many organizations make is trying to fit the new way of working into the old model. They still measure activity instead of achievement. They chase volume over value. They optimize motion, rather than impact.

In this book, we challenge that old model.

A new Productivity Mindset

Productivity for many teams is about capacity and the ability to drive meaningful outcomes. For leaders, it is about creating an environment where people have the time, tools, and clarity to do the work that truly matters. But it is also about whether doing that work is at a sustainable and high-impact pace.

Now, this does not mean that activity is irrelevant. Action matters, as mentioned before. But these must be at the service of outcomes. These must serve employee wellbeing, customer retention and loyalty, expansion, and revenue. It must serve organizational learning and growth. And remember, these also serve the individual.

For many commercial and customer-facing teams, productivity today forces us to shift from a mindset that measures "How much did we do?" to one that asks, "What did we achieve?"

This seems like a simple reframing, but it has been difficult at scale. It is too easy to fall back to our old ways. This new mindset changes what we measure.

It changes how we coach.

It changes how we design systems.

It changes how we build incentives.

It changes our tech stacks.

It changes how we enable.

It changes how we manage.

That is a lot of change, and it feels "too much, too fast". But we can focus on little pieces at a time as we build an organization that is primed for success. We cannot simply squeeze more hours or more tasks out of people. Cognitive load, emotional resilience, and personal development are now central to organizational performance.

We live in a new era. What we learned from the industrial era can help in many things, but this is a new era of capacity. And if we want to thrive, we need to build workplaces that unlock our potential, rather than exhaust or stifle it.

Activity Metrics Are Not the Enemy- Misused Activity Metrics Are

I want to make sure that I am absolutely clear. I am not advocating or calling for a world without metrics, nor am I saying activity does not matter. Of course these matter.

It matters that we have metrics, visibility, and accountability. But the wrong metrics, or even misinterpreted metrics or metrics without context, do more harm than good. We collect so much data today, teams and organizations have hundreds of data points, if not more. However, we should be careful that we aren't using data to tell a story that isn't there.

If you celebrate the number of calls made, your reps will make calls. If you reward the number of customer check-ins, your Customer Success managers will have check-ins. You will see great activity metrics. But will you see value? And will your people feel valued?

Activity has become the goal when it was meant to be the tool.

Modern leaders must focus on blended metrics like outcomes achieved, and the activities that drove them. Measured wisely and in context, activities are important leading indicators, but they are not the measure of success for a commercial team.

Instead of trying to squeeze more tasks out of each day, use the tools and capability at our disposal to increase our capacity.

- Reduce administrative drag.
- Simplify access to resources.
- Align work with clear strategic outcomes.
- Protect time for thinking, creating, and connecting.
- Free up time for high-impact & high-value work.

Technology plays a significant role in increasing our capacity. Artificial Intelligence (AI), Large Language Models (LLMs), Machine Learning (ML), Agentic AI, and traditional tools like Customer Relationship Management (CRM) and office all play very important roles (and we'll get into that in a later chapter). The point is, in commercial teams, productivity is not about activity volume. It is building capacity, activity quality, and alignment.

A high-capacity team moves fast because they are unburdened. They know where they are going, they have what they need, and they are trusted to make important decisions. These teams are coached on outcomes, not micromanaged on inputs.

This is what modern productivity looks like.

A Word on Clarity

You cannot have high productivity and capacity without clarity.

Goals must be clear, priorities must be clear, and expectations must be clear. Everyone involved must know what is important and what isn't. When this is absent, we end up wasting tons of energy. Hard-working teams end up spinning their wheels. When clarity is present, even small teams can produce massive outcomes.

Chapter Wrap

If there's one thing I hope you're taking away so far, it's this: more activity doesn't equal more value. Not anymore. Especially not in modern commercial teams where complexity, context, and collaboration matter more than sheer volume.

When we keep measuring success like we're still working an assembly line, we end up rewarding noise over traction. Teams stay busy, but they don't get better. And the real work that moves the needle gets buried under dashboards full of vanity metrics.

That's the heart of the productivity dilemma. So, what do we do with it?

Try this with your team:

- **Map:** One week of team activity to actual business outcomes. What's noise vs. traction?
- **Ask:** "Where are we working hard but not making progress?"
- **Reflect:** What metrics do we reward that don't align with results?

In the next chapter, we'll shift the conversation from output to something more powerful: capacity. Because being productive is about creating space to do the work that matters.

THE PRODUCTIVITY TRAP

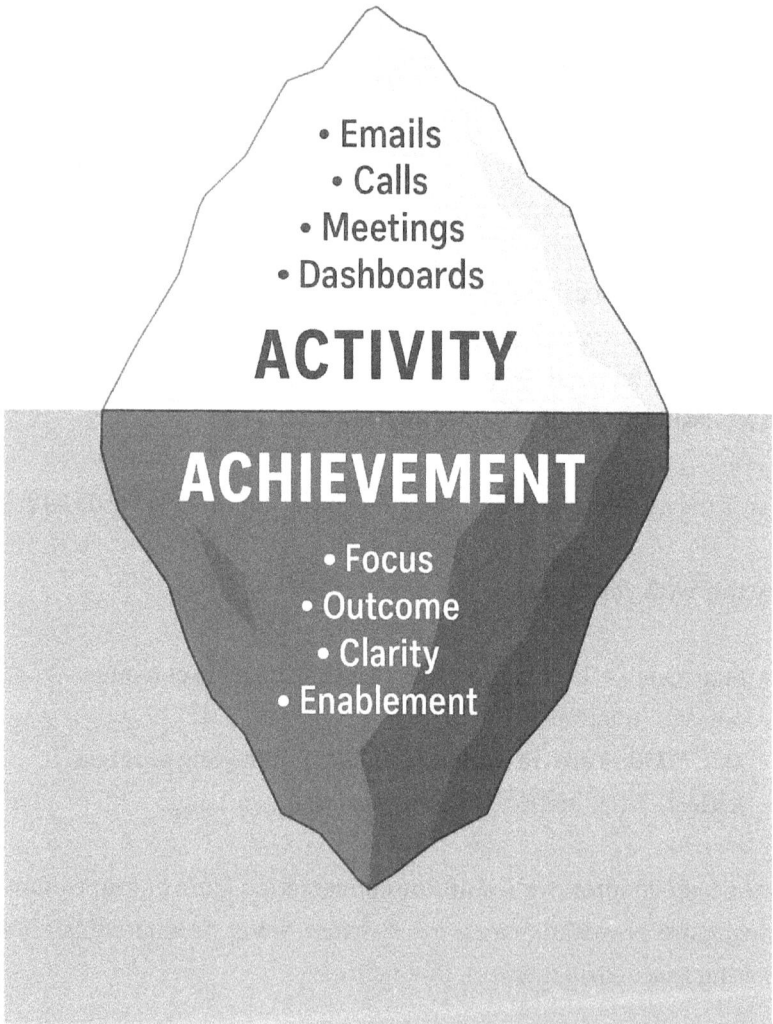

• Emails
• Calls
• Meetings
• Dashboards

ACTIVITY

ACHIEVEMENT

• Focus
• Outcome
• Clarity
• Enablement

The Productivity Trap — What's most visible isn't always what drives progress. Teams are often evaluated on surface-level activity, but the real drivers of performance live below: clarity, enablement, and outcomes.

2

Moving Beyond Output to Capacity

T eams are busier than ever but somehow getting less done. That's the trap of chasing output instead of building capacity. In this chapter, we'll reframe what productivity really means in a high-performance environment.

> "The key is not to prioritize what's on your schedule, but to schedule your priorities."
> —Stephen R. Covey

For decades, the mantra of productivity was simple.

More. More calls. More meetings. More emails. More hours.

Of course, this made sense in an industrial economy. Productivity was tangible and very visible. You needed the output from one person to complete the work of another down the assembly line. It was easy to measure.

Assemble more products. Process more orders. Ship more packages.

Clock in. Clock out. Count it all up.

The logic of productivity was binary: you either got more done or you didn't. The goal was throughput, and the tools and techniques were built around that singular idea. We designed systems, roles, and even compensation models around output. Quantity was the north star. Teams were optimized for volume and repetition, and leadership often equated more with better.

But today's work is fundamentally different. Especially in commercial roles, most of the value isn't created by sheer volume. It's created by traction, creativity, adaptability, insight, and alignment. These are not easily counted, but they're deeply felt.

There is still a place for assembly-line style processes like handoffs between sales and customer success or an Subject Matter Expert (SME) providing content for enablement to create training or product market-ing to create pitch decks. These are real, necessary motions. But they are not the bulk of the value. Output is part of the work. Outcome is the point of the work. A call doesn't matter unless it leads to progress. A meeting isn't productive unless it clears the path forward. Time spent is irrelevant if it doesn't move the needle.

And yet, many organizations cling to legacy thinking. They're still measuring productivity with a stopwatch in a world that demands a compass. Raw activity is celebrated. High volume is equated with high value. Dashboards light up with vanity metrics because they're easy to track, not because they tell us anything meaningful. It feels safer to lean on the visible, even if it's no longer valid.

But motion isn't progress. Energy isn't impact. And busyness is not the same as effectiveness. The work might be endless, but that doesn't mean it's useful. We've trained ourselves to reward action, even if that action leads nowhere. The result? Teams spend more time proving their effort than improving their effectiveness.

Look around: exhausted employees with packed calendars and little clarity. Overbuilt teams that can't move fast. Lean teams stretched so thin they can't think, let alone innovate. And what's wild is that the same disease causes both bloat and burnout. More people without more purpose only adds friction. Fewer people without better focus simply accelerates failure.

Organizations with excess headcount often fill time with busy work like extra meetings, over-polished decks, or duplicated reporting. Meanwhile, under-resourced teams run triage, unable to zoom out or solve root problems. They're constantly in reactive mode, solving the same issues repeatedly because the system can't pause long enough to rethink itself. In both cases, true productivity suffers. People aren't delivering value, they're managing chaos.

Capacity: The New Productivity Frontier

Efficiency goes beyond mere speed or output; it revolves around enhancing capacity. This concept of efficiency as capacity enhancement causes a shift in how we perceive productivity. Instead of focusing solely on the quantity of work produced, we must optimize our resources and processes to achieve better outcomes without overextending our workforce. This approach not only increases immediate productivity but also creates a sustainable work environment where employees can and want to do their best work.

Modern productivity is not simply about the volume of tasks completed, but the value that is enabled. Capacity is a combination of focus, skill, and energy carefully and thoughtfully aligned toward meaningful work.

How do you improve this ability? You must be able to do more, yes. You need to handle more tickets, juggle more demos, and deliver more sessions. There is activity there. These are all the things that need to be done. But we need to stop equating effort with effectiveness. High-capacity teams and individuals focus on working more effectively, not on working more hours. They find ways to reduce wasted time and effort, and they look for opportunities to eliminate friction.

We will talk about how to measure what matters in a later chapter, but for now, it is a good idea to think about your high-impact people and observe what they are doing. Where are they focusing time and energy? Are they circumventing certain tools or processes? If so, these might be redundant relics of your activity-focused culture.

When output is the end goal, the flywheel breaks. You start over-hiring just to drive volume. Then you under-deliver on outcomes. Then you downsize to "right-size," but the problems persist. You rehire, retool, rebuild. And none of it works because you're solving for activity instead of impact. You're solving symptoms instead of asking bigger questions. And without those bigger questions, the answers don't matter.

Your teams end up overworked, exhausted, and overwhelmed. Your systems end up inefficient, overwhelmed, and far too complicated.

It's a trap. An output trap.

The Output Trap: How Good Intentions Go Wrong

It usually begins rather innocently and with good intentions. Your leaders want results, your teams want to succeed, and everyone wants to contribute. You follow the conventional wisdom of the thought-leader because it's familiar and repeated.

Sales is a numbers game. So, you set the target for 100 cold calls per day per rep.

Marketing is about flooding the algorithm. So, you need 10 blog posts per month.

Retention is about touchpoints. So, customer success sets weekly check-ins.

The logic feels sound. And in the beginning, these metrics and activities drive action. Everyone is working more, making more calls, more posts, and more meetings. The dashboards fill up with data, and you get those beautiful pie charts and bar graphs. Everyone is busy and things are looking good.

But over time, you begin to see the shift. The metric becomes the mission. Your output is treated as the outcome. When this happens, leaders proudly report on the high activity numbers, and teams are optimizing their schedules around producing the metric. We are no longer driving sales qualifications, or product fit, or champion creation, or useful customer education and market engagement, or driving adoption of the solution. The original purpose is now gone.

Sales calls get made just to hit a quota, not to qualify or advance a deal.

Content gets published because the calendar says so, not because it's strategically useful. Check-in calls happen because they're scheduled, not because they deliver any value to the customer.

People do what's measured, not what matters.

Instead of driving for the right outcomes, teams begin to create activity for the sake of performing the activity. This creates people who are busy, but not productive. Calendars full of low-impact meetings. Sales reps working leads they know are dead just to log activity. Marketing teams publishing low-value filler content to maintain frequency. Enablement rolling out materials that collect digital dust.

It's like a treadmill. You run as fast as you can and exert a lot of energy, but you aren't going anywhere. Despite the motion and exertion, the business is not moving forward.

Real Examples, Real Tradeoffs

Imagine you run a SaaS commercial team. BDR-A sends 200 templated emails a day and books 3–5 meetings a week. BDR-B sends 50 targeted, thoughtful messages to ideal customer profiles and books the same number of meetings, but with higher potential prospects. Which rep is truly productive in a commercial revenue model?

By traditional productivity metrics, BDR-A is absolutely crushing the main metrics. Sending 200 cold emails a day, versus just 50 in a week? And I've seen so many managers look at similar BDR activity loads and ask BDR-B why they aren't contacting as many people.

They question whether time is being used effectively, and in some case, imply that it's being wasted. Even when the better outcomes are shown, while they usually soften in their tone, they continue to push for more activity—even if it may dilute the work of BDR-B.

The goal is not to send emails. The goal is to create engagement and find qualified high-potential buyers. When the metric mostly measures the motion, but not the meaning, the metric and the motion are failing.

Let's revisit the CSM example, but this time, we'll do it through the lens of outcome over output.

You have CSM-A that holds 6 check-in meetings each day, but with no agenda. Many customers are no-shows, or the calls end up being mostly small talk.

You have CSM-B who conducts 3 focused conversations each day with their accounts tied to customer-goals and expansion.

Again, by traditional metrics, CSM-A has twice as many calls with their customers each day. They are likely logging more touchpoints and more hours "worked", if you are using the calendar as evidence of working. However, the focused work from CSM B is creating more opportunities, driving more adoption, and opening opportunities for upselling and cross-selling. These fewer calls are more impactful and valuable- the outcome is greater. And you can believe that plenty of managers are having a similar conversation to our BDR manager example here. And it's undermining the CSM that is delivering tangible results.

As you consider these two examples, think about how they have a negative impact on productivity and the individuals involved. What occurs when each representative is rewarded for output rather than outcome? They begin to optimize their work to receive recognition, without considering how it impacts prospects and customers. And whether you want to admit it, the impact on customers and prospects directly affects your business and employees.

How did we get here and how do we fall into this trap so easily?

British Economist Charles Goodhart formulated his eponymous law (Goodhart's Law) in 1975, stating "when a measure becomes the target, it ceases to be a good measure". Essentially, once a metric is used as a target to make decisions, people optimize for the metric itself, and this usually happens in ways that undermine the original purpose of the metric. We see this in the examples above- chasing the metric instead of creating value.

There are plenty more examples of this in commercial teams. If a company sets a strict sales quota, employees might prioritize short-term sales at the expense of long-term customer relationships. A VP of Sales sets a demo target but does not clarify quality or buyer readiness. The Head of Marketing sets a blog quota without tying it to pipeline influence. An Enablement Director measures training sessions delivered, or new reps onboarded, but not whether skills improve.

The problem isn't that we use metrics. It's that we chase the number without the right context. We like the numbers because they are measurable, but we need to remember why we are measuring them in the first place. They need to be rooted in a strategic goal or else it becomes a vanity metric.

Burnout Is a Symptom of Misdirected Energy

Let's make it personal. Think about the times you've burned out. Was it because you had too much to do or because you were doing too much that didn't matter?

Most people don't mind working hard. They mind wasting time. They mind chasing goals that shift constantly. They mind producing work that no one uses.

That's why high-capacity cultures are intentional, not just fast. They give people permission to slow down and ask why and then reward decisions that protect energy. They invest in tools and systems that enable clarity.

They build trust by aligning the effort with the outcome. And when teams feel trusted, when they know their work matters, they lean in and become invested.

Chapter Wrap

You've probably seen it yourself: the hardest-working teams sometimes feel like they're getting nowhere. Not because they're lazy, but because they're overloaded, scattered, or stuck in systems that don't serve them.

This is what happens when we chase output and ignore capacity.

Building capacity isn't about working harder or longer. It's about removing the sludge that's made up of the admin noise, the duplicative work, and the tools nobody uses, so teams can actually move.

Try this with your team:

- **Identify:** One recurring task that drains time without delivering value.
- **Unblock:** What's getting in the way of your top performers doing their best work?
- **Reframe:** Start asking, "Does this help us deliver what matters?"

Next, we're going to talk about streamlining. But not the kind where people get laid off with a spreadsheet and a pat on the back. We'll talk about how to right-size your team and org *on purpose*.

The Output Trap Flywheel

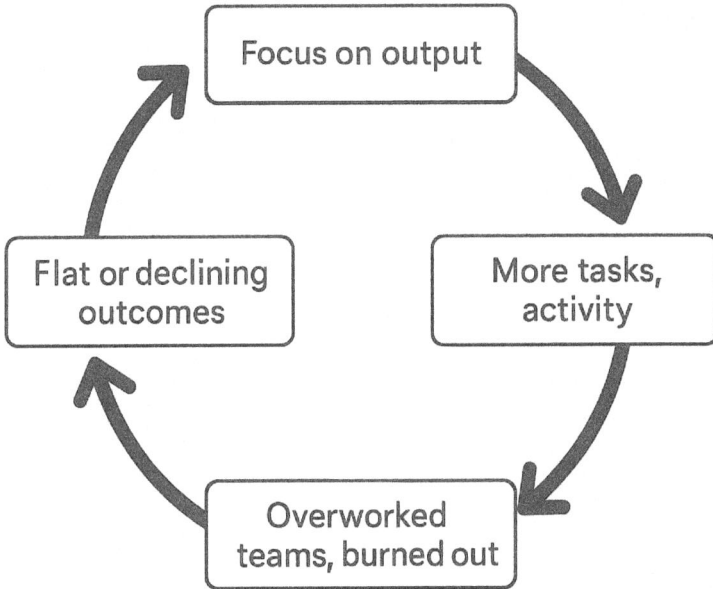

The Output Trap Flywheel — When organizations chase activity over impact, they create a self-reinforcing cycle. More output leads to more work, more burnout, and ultimately less progress — until someone breaks the loop.

3

Strategic Streamlining

S treamlining can save a business or destroy its soul. When teams are told to do more with less, most leaders reach for the same lever: cuts. But how you cut, what you cut, and what you preserve determines whether your team rebounds stronger or spirals into burnout.

"The path to success is to take massive, determined action."
—Tony Robbins

One significant flaw of the traditional model of streamlining is its reliance on metrics that prioritize speed over quality. In an effort to streamline processes, organizations often emphasize efficiency metrics like cycle time or output quantity. This narrow focus can result in a neglect of quality control, leading to increased error rates and customer dissatisfaction. When teams are pressured to produce results quickly, they may cut corners or overlook essential steps in their workflows. This not only diminishes the value of the final product or service but can also damage the organization's reputation, ultimately impacting revenue.

When financial tension mounts, and the main focus is on shareholder value, companies will often default to a simple solution. Cut costs. Cutting costs is done in several ways, but the most common are through reduced headcount, the slashing of budgets, and the elimination of programs.

Of course, the immediate savings are not only tangible, but measurable and celebrated by leadership and investors. Such austerity and acumen in the face of uncertainty and pressure.

However, these quick cuts will not solve the deeper problem. In fact, these quick cuts will often create new issues.

Reactionary streamlining often disregards the unique needs and skills of individual team members. A cookie-cutter approach to process optimization can limit employees' ability to contribute creatively to their roles. It erodes trust, destroys team capacity, hollows institutional knowledge, and creates a demoralized environment of survivor's guilt and overwhelm for those who are left.

Streamlining is important in an organization and keeps teams from becoming bloated or losing their strategic focus. But there is a vast difference between strategic streamlining and blind reactionary stream-lining. The first ends up strengthening an organization, while the latter will weaken it.

Strategic vs Blind Streamlining

Organizational capacity should match strategic priority, not be filled with busy work.

Strategic streamlining is thoughtful, intentional, and outcome driven.

It's surgical, not blunt force. It's designed to enhance long-term health, not just deliver short-term optics.

Blind streamlining is reactive, unfocused, and often panic-driven. Leadership cutting headcount or costs because "something has to give," without a clear view of what capacity will be needed afterward.

Before we dive deeper, here's the core difference to remember: *If your cuts don't reduce drag, they're likely cutting value. Strategic streamlining removes friction. Blind streamlining removes effectiveness.*

Strategic Streamlining	Blind Streamlining
Starts with clarity on core outcomes	Starts with panic about cost overruns
Involves a capacity audit	Involves blanket percentage cuts
Protects critical capabilities	Randomly damages key functions
Communicates transparently	Sows confusion and fear

Companies should look to streamline their operations and their teams, even their offerings. As companies grow too big, they begin to lose focus.

So, what does this look like in practice? Let's take two examples. One where streamlining went sideways, and another where it was done with care. Let's look at the story of StartupCo.

StartupCo is a rocket ship, one of the top SaaS platforms making noise in a competitive space. They are making money and looking to expand. They have a lot of ideas on how to integrate new features and lead the market in doing so. As they grow, they look for more investment. To show growth to investors, they hire more people and create more departments that would lead that growth. Eventually, we have StartupCo employees posting to social media their "day in the life" videos.

They would show themselves waking up, getting to the office, spending time in the lounge area, drinking free coffee, eating free meals, playing free games, and then joining 2-3 meetings. Then the afternoon would show the same.

Something very important was missing. Actual work.

"But they had meetings!" you say. Meetings are not where the work is done, I would argue. Meetings are where work is planned.

StartupCo focused on culture at the expense of the company.

They had culture but lacked capacity. People showed up, but progress didn't. They *needed* to hire more people to get the work done, not because there was too much work, but because there was not enough focus on the work.

The Board sees this issue and agrees that it is time for radical changes.

They react swiftly but without enough foresight. In trying to fix the bloat and issues, they end up undermining the very culture that supported their progress.

Now they have a new problem. They might have let go of the people who knew how to run the departments in their hurry to streamline, and those left need to quickly figure it out or build entirely new processes. The problem is they don't know how. Or they have people who know how to do the work, but they are now overworked or have too many priorities.

To fix this, leadership hires more people—and the cycle of hire and lay-off continues.

Contrast this with a mid-sized services firm—let's call it SupportWise. As demand spiked post-pandemic, they grew quickly and layered on more coordinators and project managers. But the work wasn't scaling. Instead of more outcomes, they got more meetings, more emails, and less focus. They didn't need more headcount; they needed clarity, smarter systems, and aligned incentives. When they streamlined intentionally—clarifying roles, investing in enablement, and trimming redundant tools—they saw retention rise and client results improve.

These are examples of organizational bloat that destroys productivity, and blind streamlining that cannot fix it.

These blind cuts felt fast and decisive. But they prioritized short-term gains at the expense of long-term progress.

Here's how:

- **Capacity Loss:** You lose more than just headcount. You lose knowledge, relationships, and execution muscle.
- **Morale Collapse:** Survivors suffer from "layoff survivor syndrome" and feel fear, guilt, and distrust that sap productivity for months or even years.
- **Disrupted Customer Experience:** Losing key people breaks continuity with customers, damaging trust and revenue.
- **Culture Erosion:** Layoffs done poorly signal that people are expendable. Trust decays. Engagement plummets.

In the worst cases, the very people you most need to keep are the ones who leave voluntarily after watching a blind streamlining unfold. Your adaptable, thoughtful, high-capacity employees no longer want to work at an organization that does not value them. Not only that, but they don't want to work at an organization that can so carelessly take such extreme actions in the name of the short-term.

The organization doesn't just shrink, it rots.

How Strategic Streamlining Works

But imagine if StartupCo took a more intentional path — one that prioritized strategic streamlining over panic cuts. Leadership envisioned industry dominance but understood that growth must be intentional, not just a vanity metric to impress investors.

This allowed them to make strategic additions, not reckless hires. Sometimes that meant building specialized teams for critical initiatives while keeping redundant layers lean. At other times it meant investing in technology to streamline workflows instead of relying on excessive headcount. Occasionally, it meant preserving cultural elements that reinforced productivity while eliminating distractions that drained focus.

By doing this StartupCo cultivated a culture of high performance, not excess. Employees enjoyed a positive work environment, but their productivity remained at the forefront. Meetings were purposeful and led to execution, not endless discussion. This ensured that internal expansion aligned with actual business needs.

When challenges arose, they avoided reactionary decision-making. Instead of mass layoffs or abrupt cost-cutting, they assessed where streamlining could enhance efficiency without harming execution. Adjustments were precise, preserving institutional knowledge while removing only the inefficiencies.

Strategic streamlining begins with a simple, but crucial question- "What outcomes are essential for us to survive and thrive?"

True optimization isn't about expanding recklessly or cutting blindly. Every investment should drive long-term success, whether it is in people, processes, or culture. That's the real test.

To do this, we must understand our business map's essential aspects. Strategic streamlining can't be improvised. It needs structure. Here's a simple framework to guide the process so it aligns with real business outcomes:

- Which functions are critical to those outcomes?
- Where there is duplication, drag, or bloated layers.
- Where technology or process improvement could replace low-value manual work.
- Where capabilities must be protected at all costs.

When we have this understanding, we are able to make the necessary adjustments instead of reckless reactions. This could mean cutting out redundant layers, automating administrative tasks, and even merging internal functions. We'll go deeper into how automation and AI fit into this picture in Chapter 5. For now, just know that streamlining isn't about taking things away, but it is more about making what's left work smarter.

The goal is not to cut in order to make cuts. It is not to bow down the almighty short-term. Rather, it is to optimize for strategic execution so that our time and talent drive outcomes that matter.

A common misconception with streamlining is that it means "shrinking". This is not always true. True streamlining is building a team that is appropriately sized and resourced to meet their goals. You may need to increase the size or tool stack of a team to streamline it.

This can also mean shifting focus for teams and people. As certain roles and functions are identified as redundant or even automated or augmented, redeployment of capable people to higher-impact roles and retraining them for new growth areas and opportunities is imperative.

Streamlined right-sizing is doing the right work, with the right resources.

Step	Description
Clarify Core Outcomes First	What must the company accomplish in the next 12–24 months to survive and thrive? Streamlining without this clarity is just random surgery.
Audit Capacity, Not Just Costs	Who is doing what work? Where are redundancies, low-value tasks, bottlenecks? Where is there underutilized talent that could be redeployed?
Protect Customer Impact Roles	Customer-facing roles often deliver outsized value relative to their cost. Cutting them indiscriminately harms revenue, loyalty, and brand reputation.
Communicate with Transparency and Humanity	People aren't stupid. If cuts must happen, explain the "why," the "how," and the "what next" with honesty and empathy. Silence and spin destroy trust.

Human-centered Streamlining

Many companies inadvertently add complexity. They increase management layers as they grow, create new departments without assessing the current ones, and accumulate tools and processes specific to different managers instead of establishing organizational standards.

Streamlining presents an opportunity to address these issues by flattening hierarchies, clarifying decisions, empowering teams, and improving tools and processes. It focuses on working efficiently rather than harder.

Streamlining efforts that lack adaptability can quickly become outdated. Leaders should be cautious about imposing rigid frameworks on teams, as these can hinder responsiveness to changing circumstances. Organizations should prioritize flexible capacity planning that allows for adjustments based on real-time feedback and evolving priorities.

Not everyone prefers a streamlined, high-capacity role. Some individuals favor their existing tools even if they are not optimal. Streamlining, when done correctly, can still be challenging. However, it does not need to be harsh.

Human-centered streamlining considers the impact on people's lives. Whether individuals are trained in new skills, relocated to different departments, or separated from the organization, their future differs from their past. Departures must be managed with dignity, and those remaining need clarity and reassurance in their new roles or circumstances.

Chapter Wrap

Streamlining is necessary. But too many companies confuse cost-cutting with clarity. The result? Teams lose capacity and confidence in one swoop.

We need to cut with purpose instead of panic. And we need to protect the work (and the people) that create real value.

Try this with your team:

- **Cut:** What are we doing that no longer aligns with our priorities?
- **Audit:** What tool or process added during growth is now just dead weight?
- **Reallocate:** If we had to cut 20% of effort (not people), what would we stop?

Now let's talk about the 80/20 rule. It's useful, but misused. We'll unpack how to apply it for focus — not fear.

4

Rethinking the 80/20 Rule

Most leaders misuse the 80/20 rule. They cut the bottom 80% and call it strategy. But the real power of the Pareto Principle is in what you protect. This chapter reclaims 80/20 as a tool for focus, not fear.

> "Most of us spend too much time on what is urgent and not enough time on what is important."
> —Stephen R. Covey

We talked in Chapter 2 about the trap of chasing output: how volume can create the illusion of productivity while actually draining capacity. That same logic applies here. The 80/20 rule isn't about cutting your bottom half just to lighten the load. It's about identifying where your team's real impact lives and building systems that protect and amplify it.

The 80/20 Rule, also known as the Pareto Principle, asserts that roughly 80% of effects come from 20% of the causes. This concept is particularly relevant in the context of productivity and resource management, where it serves as a guiding principle for managers seeking efficiency in their teams. By identifying the critical 20% of tasks, projects, or clients that yield the majority of results, leaders can prioritize their efforts and allocate resources more effectively. This focus not only enhances productivity but also allows teams to streamline processes and minimize waste, ultimately leading to improved performance in various workplace scenarios.

In practical applications, the 80/20 Rule can significantly impact capacity and planning. For instance, managers can analyze their workforce and determine which employees or teams are responsible for most of the output. By leveraging the strengths of these high-performing individuals, organizations can optimize their resource allocation, ensuring that the right people are focused on the most impactful tasks. This approach allows for the identification of skill gaps or areas that require additional training and end up enhancing the overall capabilities and productivity of the team.

It is a powerful concept and invites leaders to focus the energy of the team where it matters most. But like any tool, it can be dangerous when misused.

What the 80/20 Rule is Really Saying

The 80/20 rule reminds us that results will rarely match effort on a 1:1 ratio. It means that results are often unevenly distributed. And that distribution, while useful to examine, is not fixed. It's a lens, not a law.

What it does mean is that the impact you are looking for is likely to be distributed unevenly. Patterns of outsized contributions exist. But just because they exist in a certain way right now does not mean they will remain that way.

This ratio is not fixed. It is a simplification. It is dependent on input and output and will vary depending on these things. The numbers also don't need to add up to "100" since the numbers measure two different things (inputs and outcomes). Make sure that you go through your data to determine your numbers (i.e., 70/40, 90/10, 85/30).

This is directional insight—not gospel. We should use this as a signal to look deeper, not as an excuse to act rashly. In fact, when misused, bad decisions are always on the horizon.

Leaders use this rule to justify mass layoffs and keep just the "top performers". They use it as a reason to neglect employee development, ignoring potential growth for many on their teams. And they use it to oversimplify complex systems, assuming that this simple fix will be the solution to larger structural issues.

As a note, we often overlook the consistent performers outside these top 20% of people. While it is important to give top performers the right attention to keep them motivated, the middle 60% represent a significant opportunity. By providing targeted support and development opportunities, organizations can elevate the performance of this group, leading to substantial overall gains.

Here's how you can develop your middle performers in practical ways:

- **Targeted training** to build core competencies and confidence.
- **Incremental incentives** that reward improvement, not just high output.
- **Clear coaching frameworks** tied to real business outcomes.

And as productivity and outcome increase here, overall productivity and outcome increase.

How to Apply 80/20 Thoughtfully

By applying this rule in a strategic way, not a simplistic way, smart leaders and high-capacity individuals, whether leading a team or not, are able to hack their productivity.

They can recognize where outsized impact exists and harness it. They also don't treat it as a certainty that it will remain a permanent reality. Today's top performers or best engagement channels might change tomorrow due to any number of reasons. That's why they identify without idolizing the current situation. Circumstances, support, and focus can change at any moment.

They know how to develop the middle. It is by investing in coaching, training, enablement, and support for the middle 50% of people, systems, and processes. Through these seemingly small actions, we can create massive performance lifts.

They also know how to protect their strategic capacity. By staying focused on the targets and outcomes, wise stewards of the 80/20 rule never lose sight of the goal. They wonder if this focus will affect the outcomes they care about, or whether it will enable increased capacity. They use it to focus on time, process, and priority.

Thoughtful implementation forces us to focus on the outcome, not on shortcuts. This is not a way to avoid the real work of leadership and growth. The lazy practitioner wields the 80/20 rule like a blunt instrument while reminding their teams they're expendable instead of helping them grow. Or how at any moment they can simply cut the dead weight of the bottom 80% and start over.

Instead of focusing on how they can lift performance and build capacity and capability so more than succeed at a high level, they pit people and teams against each other and breed fear, instability, and turnover.

Thinking instead of the long game, leaders can build trust, growth, and sustain excellence. By improving the middle performers, everyone gets better, as do the measured outcomes. It is almost as if a rising tide can lift all boats. It will, so long as that boat is seaworthy.

Leaders in the proper mindset focus on high-value activity, develop talent, and build culture. They know that the 80/20 rule is neither a magic wand, nor a club. It is a magnifying glass that lets you find your levers and focus your intent.

Now You Increase Capacity

We've talked about the 80/20 rule and how to use it effectively. We have also talked in Chapter 2 about capacity, and the shift that needs to happen to get from an output focus to a focus on capacity building toward outcomes. But most of our discussion until now has been on why it is important to reframe our focus, instead of on what we can specifically do. So, let's take a few moments to focus on reasons and tips to help you reframe and focus based on what we've learned.

Capacity is not "how many tasks or outputs someone can complete in a single day". That is just a rebrand of output-centric activity measuring. It doesn't help anyone or fix any problems. It is just a way to claim progress.

When we build our capacity, we are not just getting more motion, we are getting better results. True capacity is focused on 4 core elements:

Core Element	Description
Focus	Directing energy toward high-impact work without distraction
Skill	Having the tools and competencies to execute effectively
Bandwidth	Protecting time and space to think, create, and perform
Resilience	Sustaining energy through challenge and change

Focus Of a Capacity-driven Organization

Capacity-driven organizations know that being obsessed with output leads to predictable problems like burnout, strategic shift, and diminishing returns. Any one of these issues can be a killer, but if you are facing all three it becomes what feels like an insurmountable task.

Burnout is the silent killer of most teams because by the time your people realize they have it, they are already suffering. They have been relentlessly chasing projects, activities, and priorities. Even the most motivated employees will fall victim to this. They do their best to "do more", but without meaning in their action, the exhaustion sets in fast.

When quantity becomes the goal, strategic priorities blur. Teams spend time on the easiest metrics to hit instead of the ones that matter most to customers and business outcomes. This strategic drift creates confusion and leads to burnout faster.

At some point, adding more calls, more meetings, or more tasks stops yielding more value. People hit a wall where more work equals less creativity, worse decision-making, and lower-quality results. Remember those all-nighters from high school or college? At some point everything just stopped making sense, and you had a terrible headache. This is usually past the point of diminishing return.

We are not infinite task machines. There are real limits to how much information we can digest in a short period of time. Limits to how many tasks we can juggle at once. And limits to the amount of stress we can absorb. Once we hit the limit one even one of these, performance falters or even collapses.

When we are constantly switching contexts, managing numerous small tasks simultaneously, and trying to keep track of information (especially when it is disorganized) our available cognitive capacity is drained. And that's before we even start on the most important work. Unfortunately, the mental effort required to complete a task is too-often overlooked when designing work and teams.

Smart leaders recognize that you cannot brute-force human output forever. You must design systems that respect and extend human capacity. They need to consider cognitive load.

They help their teams to structure work into focused blocks or at least protect focus-time on their calendars. Teams are starting to automate repetitive administrative tasks with AI and workflows so they can prioritize high-impact and high-value work. These leaders also ensure clarity and simplicity in their communication and expectations, and make themselves available to discuss, remove roadblocks, and advocate for the programs, projects, and people that make up their high-performing team.

Capacity expands naturally when organizations eliminate friction and promote focus. Think about reducing or eliminating these top areas where friction is created:

- **Administrative Drag:** Endless forms, manual data entry, duplicative approvals.
- **Tool Sprawl:** Too many platforms, too many logins, too much noise.
- **Meeting Creep:** Meetings without agendas. Meetings that could have been emails. Meetings about meetings.
- **Content Confusion:** Wasting time searching for resources, templates, or data.

Here's how modern organizations can build capacity instead of just chasing output:

Action	Why It Matters
Clarify Strategic Priorities	Everyone should know what the "big rocks" are — the few key outcomes that matter most this quarter, this year, this cycle.
Audit Workflows Ruthlessly	Look for wasted effort, duplication, and friction. Simplify where possible. Automate where appropriate.
Invest in Enablement	Give people the tools, skills, and systems they need to operate at a higher level — not just faster, but smarter.
Protect Deep Work	Schedule blocks of uninterrupted work time. Encourage asynchronous communication when real-time isn't necessary. Respect people's time and attention.
Measure Outcomes, Not Just Activity	Track progress against meaningful goals, not just checklists. Celebrate impact achieved, not just hours worked.
Build in Recovery	Recognize that sustained high performance requires rest, reflection, and learning cycles. Recovery isn't a luxury. It's part of capacity building.

Chapter Wrap

The 80/20 rule is not a hammer, nor is it a license to fire your bottom 80% and call it a strategy. The real question is: what 20% of your work, people, or processes drive disproportionate value? And how do you protect that?

Try this with your team:

- **Analyze:** What 20% of your work drives 80% of value?
- **Develop:** What support would lift your middle performers one level higher?
- **Challenge:** Are we cutting smart or just cutting fast?

Next up: AI, automation, and the myth that you can just tech your way to better productivity. Spoiler alert: you can't. But you can use it to expand capacity if you do it right.

THE CAPACITY CORE

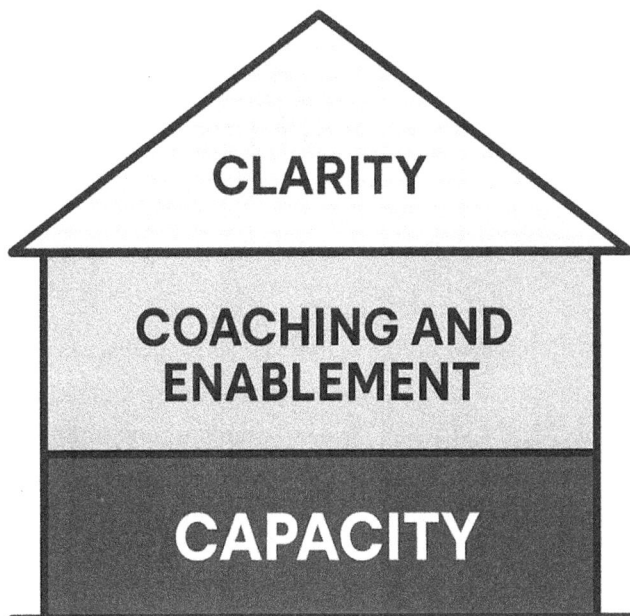

The Capacity Core — Sustainable team performance is built on a strong foundation. Capacity allows for focus and endurance. Coaching and enablement provide the support. Clarity gives direction. Together, these create the conditions for better work at scale.

5

AI, Automation, and Human Capacity

A I won't replace your team, but it will reveal where your systems are broken. The real question is how to use it to unlock human capacity. In this chapter, we'll explore how to apply AI with intention, so your people can spend more time on what matters most.

> "It is not the strongest of the species that survives, nor the most intelligent. It is the one most adaptable to change."
> —**Charles Darwin** (attributed)

Technological advancements used to occur far less frequently than they do now. The first significant advancements were things like fire, the wheel, and agriculture. These innovations allowed humans to cook food and have light at night, travel more efficiently, and cultivate crops, leading to development of stable communities and civilizations.

Thousands of years later, we began innovating faster. The printing press revolutionized the way information was circulated, making knowledge more accessible and improving literacy and education for everyone. This was followed by the radio and telephone, which connected people across vast distances, enabling instant communication and the sharing of ideas that used to take weeks or months via ship and horseback.

The invention of the car and airplane then transformed transportation, making it possible to travel quickly and efficiently. The television brought entertainment and news into people's homes, helping to shape public opinion and culture.

The computer and internet ushered in the digital age, revolutionizing every aspect of life from work to social interactions. Information is more readily available than ever before. People are more connected than ever before.

How do you feel that each of these eras was received? Every technological advancement was met with varying degrees of excitement, skepticism, and reluctance. In many cases, they were also met with fear.

Now, we are entering the era of Artificial Intelligence (AI), which is transforming the way we live and work by automating tasks, providing insights, and enhancing decision-making processes. AI has the potential to solve complex problems, improve efficiency, and create new possibilities for innovation.

And we are currently in that moment of excitement, skepticism, and fear. We need to greet opportunities and advancements with healthy doses of optimism and skepticism. Optimism to see the opportunities that are available, and skepticism so that we can avoid misinformation and bias.

You can feel it everywhere. News stories, articles, social media posts on how this is amazing, scary, game-changing, and a fad. Unreliable companies white-labeling junk apps to make a quick buck in the AI gold rush will leave a lot of people with a bad taste in their mouths. They will confirm the suspicions of many skeptics. But this is not new, bad actors flock to ever emerging markets and opportunities. Even the best-intentioned will make mistakes as we work through this new era of technology and innovation.

Some of these fears are valid, of course. There will be a shift in the way a lot of people will work, and that will require up-skilling and changing of focus. We will need to deal with these buzzwords flooding corporate decks, business-speak, and thought-leader guru posts. And we will have endless debates on how AI will replace everyone in all industries.

Anxiety is valid but misses a critical aspect. The future of work is not human OR machine. It is more likely to be human *and* machine. AI won't simply replace jobs. It transforms how work itself is done for many roles. It will shift the focus of what humans do and what AI does. It will create new opportunities for growth as it also removes opportunities.

AI will redefine productivity and capacity. Much of the current usefulness of AI is in agents and workflow optimization, allowing humans to focus on more valuable actions. Currently, most of the AI agents and bots from 2024-2025 are still focused on outputs like cold calls and emails, but it is only a matter of time until they are better aligned to outcomes.

Replace or Enhance?

In most cases, the opportunity is not to compete with AI, it is to partner with it to enhance our capacity. Not that you would see that in the current discourse. Most conversations end up in two extremes.

Mindset	Description	Risk
Replacement	*Machines take over everything, making humans obsolete*	*Fear, inaction, resistance*
Enhancement	*Machines automate drudge work; humans focus on high-value work*	*Naïve utopianism*

Most teams will land somewhere in the middle. But those who actively design for enhancement will outperform those who reactively brace for replacement. Think back to Chapter 3, where we talked about how streamlining is not a blunt instrument, but a strategic rebalancing of time, tools, and talent. AI, when used wisely, is one of the most powerful tools we have for strategic streamlining. Not to replace people, but to reduce drag and sharpen focus so your people can spend time where it matters.

Some tasks have already shifted to AI, and that shift will become permanent soon (if it hasn't already). And it should be welcome. For over 15 years I have heard from sales reps how they hate the repetitive and time-consuming administrative tasks of updating the CRM. You can now have an AI Agent scrape your call recording and email and then ask your approval to make the necessary CRM updates.

For years we have been talking about wasted time, how sellers and customer success reps spend too much time on these tasks and not enough driving actual results. They need to do the task so we can measure the growth, but doing the task takes away time from is truly valuable. Now we can use AI to automate a lot of these workflows.

That's just the tip of the iceberg. AI is replacing and augmenting high-repetition, low complexity tasks like:

- Data entry and manual record-keeping.
- Basic scheduling and calendar management.
- Routine customer service inquiries (chatbots, self-service portals).
- Information retrieval and simple lookup tasks.
- Basic order-taking (in fast food, retail, admin settings).
- First-pass resume screening and form processing.

These predictable and repeatable actions are exactly where AI thrives right now. Organizations should plan and expect for these adjustments, then invest appropriately. The need for humans is still there, someone needs to build or maintain these agents and workflows.

AI-Enhanced Capacity

While some tasks are disappearing, far more roles are currently being enhanced and augmented by AI.

As this book is focused on commercial teams, let's look at some key examples in commercial teams where this is the case. Situations where AI lowers the floor by automating tasks, allowing humans to raise the ceiling and focus on strategic actions.

Function	What AI Handles	What Humans Focus On
Sales Dev (BDR)	Prospect research, outreach drafting	Live conversations, qualifying, championing
Customer Success	Basic support, churn risk alerts	Strategic guidance, renewal and expansion
Enablement	Summarizing calls, organizing playbooks	Coaching, program design, skills development
Leadership	Dashboards, data synthesis	Decision-making, people development

Treating AI as a teammate instead of a threat requires a mindset shift, not just individually, but across the organization. AI isn't magic. These tools are effectively pattern recognition at a scale beyond human capacity. Leveraging that, and combining it with human skills like creativity, empathy, adaptability, critical thinking, and strategic alignment will allow for the true revolution where AI and people are working intelligently together.

The pragmatic, yet visionary, leader who is looking to augment their team with AI would do well to remember this and implement these basic strategies for working alongside AI:

Understand What AI Can and Cannot Do	Leaders must demystify AI for their teams. It's pattern recognition at scale.
Focus on Complementary Skills	Humans must double down on uniquely human strengths: Empathy, Creativity, Adaptability, Critical thinking, Strategic judgment
Train for AI Collaboration	AI requires onboarding. Teach employees how to integrate AI outputs thoughtfully into their workflows.
Encourage AI-Assisted Experimentation	Teams should be encouraged to find new ways to use AI. They should not fear punishment for trying and iterating.

Leadership in this emerging world will flourish or falter based on whether they resist or embrace this technology. They must realize that technology, even AI, serves people. It is not the other way around.

AI is beginning to, and will continue to, be embedded in daily work. The successful modern leader will:

- **Champion Augmentation Over Replacement:** Make it clear that AI's role is to enhance, not eliminate, human potential.

- **Redefine Productivity Metrics:** Move beyond activity counts toward impact-based measures (value created, problems solved, relationships built).
- **Invest in Human Development:** As AI manages more baseline work, humans must be continuously upskilled for higher-order contributions.
- **Lead Through Change with Empathy:** Remember that change triggers fear. Transparent communication, open forums, and a learning-oriented culture are critical during AI transitions.
- **Architect Hybrid AI Systems:** Do not be tied to one type of solution. Be open to using local models and RAG (Retrieval-Augmented Generation) for high-frequency and repeatable execution that feed into traditional LLMs for more complex, strategic tasks.

The role of AI and automation in modern workplaces is pivotal in shaping the future of work. By streamlining processes, enhancing capacity planning, and fostering collaboration between humans and machines, organizations can achieve significant gains in productivity and efficiency. For managers, commercial teams, and revenue teams, understanding and embracing these technologies is not merely an option but a necessity for maintaining competitiveness in an increasingly dynamic business environment. As the landscape continues to evolve, those who effectively leverage AI and automation will be better positioned to thrive and drive sustainable growth.

Chapter Wrap

AI is a great tool, but it's not magic. It won't fix bad processes or bad management. But used wisely, it can reduce drag and free your team to do higher-value work.

This isn't about replacing people. It's about making space for judgment, creativity, and strategy by letting tech handle the tedious stuff.

Try this with your team:

- **Eliminate:** What task do you dread weekly that a tool could do better?
- **Surface:** Where do we need better insight faster, and could AI help?
- **Evaluate:** Are we using tech to extend strengths, or just adding noise?

AI is one of the most powerful technologies we've ever had access to, but it's still just one part of the larger tech ecosystem most teams work in every day. And while AI might be new and exciting, most teams are still buried in tools they don't use, dashboards they don't trust, and workflows that slow them down. Let's look at how to build a tech stack that actually supports focus, not just adds friction.

6

Tools & Tech That Actually Matter

Y*our tech stack should make work easier. But most teams are buried under tools they don't use and dashboards they don't trust. This chapter is about cutting through the noise: how to choose tools that amplify your team, not distract them.*

> *"Technology is best when it brings people together."*
> —**Matt Mullenweg**

It has never been easier to buy tools for your business. You have solutions for everything, and you even have solutions without problems. You can get a tool for communication, project management, forecasting, sales automation, engagement, enablement, analytics, you name it!

Every one of these tools promises to be a solution for you, and a benefit to your productivity. They all promise to streamline your processes. Every demo even showed beautiful dashboards or smooth workflows with clean data.

And yet, despite all of this technology, many teams are feeling more overwhelmed and even fatigued.

The natural next step is to go find yet another tool to solve this new problem caused by all the tools. But the problem isn't technology and tools. The problem is how we adopt it, integrate it, and use it.

Buying more tech doesn't make you more productive. It often fractures capacity, distracts focus, and masks deeper issues of alignment. Tools should increase clarity and enable high-impact work. Otherwise, they waste time and dilute your organization's ability to deliver outcomes that matter. We don't always need a good, or even great, tool. We need the right tool. The right tools will reduce friction, increase focus, and amplify our strengths.

Think back to Chapter 2, where we talked about building capacity by reducing friction. Or Chapter 4, where we used 80/20 thinking to focus on what drives real results. The same logic applies here: your tools should not be features on a budget line. They should be force multipliers.

If a tool does not make work easier, clearer, and more impactful then it isn't helping. And as we discussed in Chapter 5, AI and automation only deliver value when they're embedded thoughtfully into human systems. If you drop smart tech into a broken process, it just creates faster chaos. The tool isn't the problem. The use case (or more fittingly, the lack of one) is. This is a hard reality to face. The reality is that we are drowning in solutions that actually cause more problems. So many tech stacks are creating noise, bloating your budgets, and causing distraction from the work our teams should be focused on.

Tool Fatigue

I remember working with a tech startup years ago that took pride in having "all of the best tools". This is a common pitfall, especially in startups, where teams are basically told to do whatever it takes to grow. Departments go out with big budgets to invest in the hot new solution that everyone is either posting about or is top rated on the review boards. In many cases, they go out and get one that they have personal experience with and bring into their team.

This almost unchecked implementation of different solutions often leads to what I like to call "tool fatigue". This is when, despite having the "best-in-class" tools, teams find themselves overwhelmed and less efficient because they have too many tools to manage.

The allure is, of course, undeniable. Each tool on its own usually offers superior functionality, innovative features, and the promise of enhanced efficiency. However, when these tools are obtained and deployed in a vacuum, rather than part of a larger ecosystem, they can create more problems than they solve.

You wind up spending too much time on interoperability and maintenance than getting the tool to actually work. You wind up with 4 serious issues:

Issue	Description
Fragmented Workflows	Teams juggle multiple tools with different interfaces, logins, and learning curves, disrupting workflow and increasing time spent switching.
Redundant Data Entries	Without integration, information needs to be entered multiple times across platforms, wasting time and increasing error risk.
Inconsistent User Experience	Different tools have different user experiences and interfaces, making adaptation challenging and decreasing productivity.
Increased Learning Curve	Each new tool introduces a learning curve, making training time-consuming and costly.

In the case of the startup I was at, they created fragmented workflows and redundant data entry. Even though they were using the tools deemed the absolute best in their respective spaces, the teams were not using them. I noticed it when talking to the reps because we couldn't find accurate data to populate the built-in dashboards. It turns out everyone was simply using spreadsheets saved to their own cloud drive to hold the info and then running reports and updates from there.

When I asked why, they said that these tools were "nice", but they needed to enter the same information 3 or more times to populate everything. So, they just used spreadsheets for data, and the CRM for notes, then prayed they had all the answers.

Their best tools became a time sink, a point of contention, and a waste of massive amounts of money. In fact, if you need to find a budget, look at your tech stack and find redundancy or unused solutions—you'll often find that redundancy is hiding in plain sight.

Choosing the Right Tools

The best tech setups almost feel invisible. They can seamlessly blend in and support the work we do without overwhelming or aggravating us. If you are constantly talking about your solutions and brainstorming how to get everyone to use them correctly, then you might need to have a conversation about whether it is the right tool first. When technology is working well, people don't talk about it constantly.

Most organizations fall into the same snares when adding technology. We talked about some of it earlier, but these five traps are the most common:

1. **Tool Overload** - Adding tool after tool without considering overlap, complexity, or adoption burden.
2. **Lack of Integration** - Tools that don't communicate with each other create silos, forcing users into manual workarounds.
3. **Chasing Trends** - Buying technology based on hype, not actual strategic need.
4. **Ignoring User Experience** - Selecting tools based on features, not how intuitive and accessible they are for real users.
5. **Underestimating Change Management** - Assuming that simply purchasing a tool will drive behavior change without training, support, or cultural alignment.

Falling victim to these issues creates process debt where extra layers of work are required just to manage the tools themselves. Think about how many people you have in an operations team that are specifically hired to make sure tools work together and don't break. Or even better, do you have full-time employees that are dedicated to a single tool?

So how do we ensure that we are adopting the right technology? This is different for each team or organization and based on many elements. But you can get a good idea if you take a look at several factors.

1. **Strategic Alignment.** Perhaps the most important consideration is how closely this tool will align with your strategic focuses and goal. Does this tool help us achieve a defined, meaningful business outcome? Or is it solving an invented problem?
2. **Ease of Use.** One of the biggest barriers to use is how hard it is to change the way we work. Will the average user find it intuitive? Or will it require constant handholding, workarounds, and frustration?
3. **Integration Potential.** Usually top-of-mind for the Ops departments, does it connect easily with the tools and systems we already use? Or does it create another silo?
4. **Adoption Energy.** This is tied closely to ease of use. How much cultural change, training, and reinforcement will be needed for real adoption? Is the juice worth the squeeze?
5. **Time to Value.** How quickly will users see tangible benefits from using the tool?

If we are looking across these criteria and there are major red flags or low scores here, it might be the best idea to move forward, regardless of how flashy the demo was, how persuasive the vendor is, or the internal pressures. Great tools in isolation might not be the best tools for you when integrated.

Focusing on What Matters

We all know that not all tools are created equal. Certain categories of tools consistently show strong returns when thoughtfully selected and implemented. Making sure that you have these important solutions in place correctly will go a long way in enhancing your team's capability and capacity.

I will mention the names of some tools here, but this is not an endorsement of any tool over another. And if I fail to mention one, it is not a negative endorsement.

- **Collaboration and Communication Platforms-** Slack, Microsoft Teams, Zoom. These platforms reduce email volume and enhance real-time or asynchronous collaboration.
- **CRM and Customer Intelligence-** Salesforce or HubSpot, and Zoom-Info or Apollo. Properly configured, these systems centralized customer data and actionability.
- **Enablement and Content Access-** Seismic, HighSpot, SalesHood. These tools ensure reps can easily find and deploy the right materials at the right time.
- **Conversation Intelligence and Analytics-** Gong, Chorus. These AI-driven call analysis platforms surface coaching moments, competitive trends, and customer sentiment faster than manual review.
- **AI Summarization and Workflow Automation-** AI overlays that automatically summarize meetings, suggest next actions, and organize information for faster follow-up.
- **Project and Task Management-** Asana, Monday.com, ClickUp. These tools make team progress visible, accountable, and manageable without endless check-in meetings.

The tools that succeed, and the categories that matter most all have something in common. These aren't just activity trackers. Although you can set them up and run them in that way, they are designed for greater performance. When aligned to strategic business goals, thoughtfully integrated together, and within your team processes, these tools provide clarity and focus, as well as enhance execution.

The Tech Tool Bottom Line

Ultimately, tools are purchased and implemented to serve a purpose. If it adds more work than it saves, then it is a failure. Buying the tool is easy. In most cases, it is far too easy. It is the integration into workflows that is the real challenge.

Smart integration means embedding technology into existing workflows in a way that adds as few steps as possible. It means training users in context of the tool and process so they can understand and appreciate the flow. It is measuring adoption early and often and giving opportunities for champions to stand up and talk about their best practices and quick wins to get the team encouraged. But it also means decommissioning redundant, low-usage, or unnecessary tools, regardless of the optics.

When you've built a great tech stack, it becomes an extension of how your teams already (or need to) work. You are intentionally designing systems to protect time, enhance creativity and collaboration, and reduce administrative burden. Great approaches enable better and faster decision-making by showing the metrics that matter and surfacing leading indicators for good and bad outcomes. This allows high-impact work to scale without the burnout of activity-focused tool lift.

Chapter Wrap

Tech should make your team stronger. The problem isn't too few tools. It's too many tools doing too little of what matters. And every new tool adds complexity if it doesn't solve a real problem.

Try this with your team:

- **List:** What tools do we have that no one really uses?
- **Spot:** Where are people bypassing systems for spreadsheets or workarounds?
- **Streamline:** Are we tracking performance in five places just to say we are?

Next up: We'll dig into what we measure and why it matters more than almost anything else. Because the wrong metric, even with the right tool, still drives the wrong behavior.

Tool Stack Scorecard/ Audit Matrix

Evaluate the tools in your stack by how they impact clarity, capacity, and outcomes – not just their features.

	Clarity	Capacity	Outcomes
Clear			
Fine			
Foggy			
Jammed			

Rigorous tools that clutter the user experience lead to jammed processes. A "fine" tool that is simple to use leads to greater focus and therefore better outcomes.

Tool Stack Scorecard / Audit Matrix — *Evaluate tools by the clarity they provide, the capacity they create, and the outcomes they support — not just by features or trendiness.*

7

Measuring the Right Things

I f you measure the wrong thing, you incentivize the wrong behavior. Output is easy to track, but outcome is what drives growth. In this chapter, we'll redefine productivity metrics so they reflect what really matters: impact, alignment, and results.

"What gets measured gets managed."
—Peter Drucker

In the earliest days of work, "productivity" was straightforward. Hunt more. Build more. Harvest more. If you stacked more hay, caught more fish, or shaped more arrowheads, you were productive.

Then came factories.

As the industrial age took hold, productivity became a numbers game. Machines rolled out goods. Humans were timed, tracked, and tallied. Metrics like units produced, hours worked, and errors made became standard. It made sense because these were jobs with linear inputs and clear outputs. More effort, more product.

But while the nature of work has changed, our way of measuring work has not.

Now in offices and on Zoom calls, coworking spaces and cloud-based dashboards, we still find people being judged by volume instead of value. How many calls did you make? How many tickets did you close? How many emails did you send? These numbers are tidy and convenient. They are easy to put on a slide.

But easy doesn't mean useful. In fact, in knowledge work, these old-school metrics are often actively misleading because the reality is that output is not the same as outcome.

We often either confuse the two or actively conflate them. The problem in doing this is that we not only waste time, but we also end up designing entire systems that reward the wrong behavior.

Quantity Over Quality? Be Careful What You Reward

Let's be honest for a minute, everyone we know loves a clean dashboard. It feels good to look at a leaderboard and see numbers tick upward or have great pie charts and bar graphs. It feels tidy and rewarding.

But the catch with this is that what gets measured gets managed, and what gets rewarded gets repeated. If we tell sales reps they'll be judged on calls made, they'll make more calls regardless of quality. If we track customer success by "meetings held," we'll get more meetings even if the customer would rather have a concise email. If we push marketing to hit a quota of content assets, they'll crank them out even if engagement drops and nobody reads past the headline.

In doing this, our metrics start to shape our reality. This doesn't happen because they are accurate, though. It happens because they are getting a response. Leadership and teams are responding to the data, whether it is useful or not. And it happens repeatedly in companies that track activity to the decimal while missing the bigger picture. We mistake being busy for being effective and celebrate volume over value.

Nothing will burn out your good people faster than working hard on the wrong things.

Let's put it this way: how an organization measures work is one of the clearest signals of what it values. It sets the tone for what matters, and over time, those signals shape the culture.

It's obvious when it is written down or said aloud. If your team feels like every minute is being watched, every click is being counted, every call is being logged they learn that presence matters more than progress, activity matters more than results, and perhaps most dangerously, that compliance is more valuable than creativity. This kind of culture doesn't inspire people to solve hard problems; it teaches them to play a game. If your culture is one of checking boxes, then do not be upset that you have box-checkers instead of innovators.

To move forward, we must untangle two concepts that often get lumped together—output and outcome. We've talked about it earlier, but let's clear it again, mainly because this is the most important understanding in this entire book. In fact, it is the crux of the book itself—moving from output to outcome.

Output is determined by activity metrics, which measure what and how much people *do*.

Outcome is determined by metrics that measure what *happens as a result* of outputs.

Activity is often a leading indicator. It is a signal that work is happening, but it's not the work itself. It is an easy way to see that some sort of effort has been put forth. But the business actually depends on the outcome. This is what grows and sustains the company.

And to be clear, both have an important place in management and measurement. But we need to use them wisely.

Bad Metrics in the Wild

Let's walk through a few examples that might hit a little too close to home:

- **Sales:** A rep is praised for logging 100 cold calls a day. But those calls are rushed, unresearched, and rarely lead to qualified meetings. Meanwhile, a quieter rep who does deep research, customizes their pitch, and books fewer but stronger meetings gets less recognition — even though their pipeline converts better.
- **Customer Success:** A CSM is encouraged to "touch" every account weekly. So, they flood inboxes with check-in emails that feel generic and forced. Customers stop responding, but hey — the activity number looks great.
- **Marketing:** A team is told to publish three new assets a week. Quality drops. Engagement drops. But the content calendar is full, so the box is checked.
- **Enablement:** An enablement leader is celebrated for hosting four training sessions a month. But no one measures whether those sessions actually improved rep performance.

This is the measurement trap. It's what happens when we reward volume in a vacuum.

So how do we fix it?

First, we ask better questions. Here are four that should become standard whenever designing a metric:

1. **Does this metric correlate with something we truly care about?** If not, why are we tracking it?
2. **Will this metric drive the right behavior?** Or are we accidentally rewarding the wrong things?
3. **Is it clear and understandable to the people being measured?** Confusion breeds disengagement.
4. **Can it be influenced through daily work?** If not, it's not a fair or useful metric.

Next, we start aligning metrics with the strategic goals of each team. For example:

Department	Track	Not Just
Sales	Opportunity progression, deal size growth, revenue closed per rep	Calls made or emails sent
Customer Success	Net revenue retention (NRR), churn reduction, customer health improvements	Meetings held
Marketing	Pipeline influenced, campaign conversion rates, engagement per asset	Assets created
Enablement	Time-to-productivity, skill development based on performance, ramp speed	Training sessions hosted
Leadership	Strategic goal completion, employee engagement, team health	Projects launched or hours logged

Each of these shifts the focus from activity to impact. From "Did we do it?" to "Did it work?"

If you're thinking about where to focus measurement energy, Chapter 4's take on the 80/20 rule is a useful lens. What 20% of activities or contributors are actually driving outcomes? That's where your metrics should live — not across every possible action, but at the leverage points.

The Power of Qualitative Insights

Of course, not everything can be captured in a spreadsheet. Metrics are only part of the story. They're data points. While they are useful, they are incomplete. The human side of work requires the context of qualitative inputs. It can come across as soft data, but many times this is where the important insights come from.

- A 1:1 where a rep shares how they're really feeling.
- A customer call where subtle feedback reveals dissatisfaction.

- An internal Slack thread that surfaces friction between departments.
- An exit interview that reveals systemic issues no dashboard ever caught.

Even when your metric looks great, if your team is burnt out you have a problem. If your churn rate is low but your customers are resentful, you're sitting on a time bomb. If your employee survey scores look fine but no one feels safe being honest, you're not measuring reality. And the best leaders know how to read between the lines. They treat data as conversation starters, not conversations themselves.

At its best, measurement builds trust. When used with care, it helps teams understand where they stand, gives leaders visibility into progress, and makes conversations about performance fair and constructive. Used poorly, metrics can do the opposite. They create fear, resentment, and cynicism while turning work into a game of optics.

That means when someone misses a number, we get curious and ask why, instead of getting upset and leveling accusations. When a metric goes south, we look for patterns so we can understand the issues, instead of looking for scapegoats to blame and push the real problem down the road. And when a team struggles, we offer support to identify what is going wrong, and what is going right.

Great leaders take the data and build a personalized coaching plan for their teams. Great cultures use metrics to find best practices and trends and then use them to spark growth and reward key players. If you or your leaders hide behind data or use it as a club to punish teams, then you need to rethink the "great workplace culture" you might claim.

It is also important to remember that metrics shouldn't be permanent.

They should be able to evolve as we grow and adapt and understand our people, processes, and customers more. What made sense at one stage of growth may not work at another. A startup tracking everything by hand may eventually need smarter dashboards. A mature company with rigid OKRs might need to reintroduce flexibility.

The world changes. Markets shift. Customer expectations rise. We must keep asking:

- Are we measuring the right things?
- Are we over-measuring the wrong ones?
- Are we creating the behavior we want?

We are in a world that is increasingly shaped by data, and now it is even shaped by AI. Most AI tools today brag about "doing more." It's an SDR bot that never sleeps and sends 2000 emails. While there is value to increased activity, the real opportunity of AI isn't just speed or volume. The real opportunity is clarity, insight, and precision.

With AI-enhanced dashboards, we can track not just who *did something*, but what *worked*. And after tracking that we can begin to gather insight into why it worked and then look for ways to replicate it across the team. We can connect activity to results with greater fidelity.

We can spot trends earlier, understand impact faster, and coach smarter.

We become what we measure. We become what we measure. So, if you measure speed, you'll get haste; if you measure volume, you'll get noise; but if you measure alignment, impact, and quality then you'll build teams that pursue excellence.

Measurement isn't just about accountability. It's also about direction. So, choose wisely and measure with care.

Great data is imperative to great decision-making, but it isn't the only thing to look at. Data-only analysis leaves out key components of the emotional reason people act how they do. If you only look at data for customers, you won't see the full picture of why they are a customer.

That being said, we need to collect, refine, and understand data. When we are trying to enhance productivity and optimize resources, leveraging the right data helps you gain valuable insight. This insight gives you a deeper view into how to build strategy that matters.

We've covered some of the great data points we need to measure, but your organization might have others. What is important to remember is that having 100 or even a thousand data points might sound impressive and helpful, but if you cannot tie that data to something meaningful, it is just noise.

Chapter Wrap

To be honest, we love metrics that look good on slides. Call counts, open rates, "time in seat." But that's not the point. Metrics should tell us if we're actually making progress, not just if we're busy.

Try this with your team:

- **Challenge:** Which of our "sacred" metrics don't reflect real progress?
- **Align:** Are we rewarding volume or value?
- **Refocus:** What's one outcome we want? Do our metrics support it?

Next up: You've got the metrics. Now how do you actually implement change that sticks? Let's talk about rollouts, buy-in, and the human side of doing things differently.

Measurement Ladder

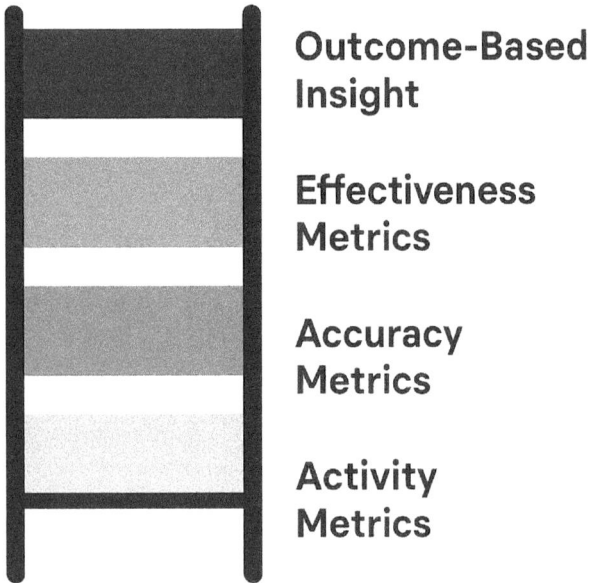

Outcome-Based
Insight

Effectiveness
Metrics

Accuracy
Metrics

Activity
Metrics

Most commercial teams are stuck
here — the reinvention is moving up

The Measurement Ladder — *Many teams stop at tracking activity. But real progress comes from moving up the ladder toward clarity, effectiveness, and outcome-based insight.*

8

Implementing Change Thoughtfully

Y ou can have the right idea and still fail if your rollout breaks trust. Implementing change requires you to create clarity, confidence, and buy-in. This chapter is your guide to building change that sticks.

"The cost of being wrong is less than the cost of doing nothing."
—Seth Godin

Change initiatives often start with the best of intentions. Teams are rolling out a new tool to help streamline work, new metrics focus on outcomes, or new systems are introduced to enhance collaboration. But the good ideas and objectives are not enough to get a change to stick.

Think back to a change initiative you've gone through. A common personal one is working to become healthier. All the doctors in the world can tell you about eating well and exercising. But, for me, it's chocolate. All the knowledge about what is right, and even the intention to change didn't get me to do it.

Business changes are similar. Our output metrics are like chocolate. We get a great instant dopamine hit, but the outcome is tomorrow's problem. Most change efforts don't fail because they are wrong, they fail because they are rushed. Leadership has a knee-jerk reaction and need to make sweeping changes right away to save the quarter. Teams are left with no context or understanding, little training (if any), and no support. Even leadership might now know why the change is happening, just that it needs—usually to placate an investor.

We then implement new metrics but will often leave behind the meaningful measures while we focus on the short-term output to fix it all. But the problem is that when change feels sudden, top-down, and unexplained we put up barriers. Even if something good is coming. The thing is, most people recognize when things are not working, but continue because it is easier—like eating chocolate.

We view the act of change as an operational issue and often overlook the deeply emotional aspect of making meaningful change. We ignore the human side and fail to get the initiatives to stick. You need to balance the right amount of logic and emotion. Too much logic and we don't feel the push to change. Too much emotion and we don't why we need to.

When we make changes poorly, the fallout is immense and fast. People push back openly against new systems they don't trust. They resist quietly in their daily work as well. Teams waste energy trying to figure out what is happening, or even how to implement the change requested. They argue about why it is even necessary. New tools and processes go unused while the rushed training is quickly forgotten and ends up gathering dust.

Poor implementation weakens the very foundation of a high-performance culture, leading to cynicism as trust erodes, money is squandered, and productivity wasted. We saw something similar in Chapter 3 with blind streamlining. When leaders make cuts or changes without clarity, they erode trust and capacity in one move. Implementation and streamlining are two sides of the same coin: both must be intentional to work.

Successful Change Enablement

Now think back to a change you wanted to make that was successful. Chances are, it didn't succeed because it was flawless out of the gate. It likely worked because the team was aligned before it was activated, because communication was thoughtful and ongoing, and because the people impacted were empowered to adopt it.

In other words: clarity, communication, and enablement.

Great alignment comes from being anchored to a clear "why". This allows teams to not only understand *what* is changing, but also to understand *why it matters.* It ties this need for change to themselves, to their daily work, to their customers, and to the company's future.

Change requires more than announcements and bullet points. It requires compelling communication through storytelling.

When I say "storytelling", what is the first thing you think of? Most people think of childhood tales, or a great movie plot. But at its core, storytelling is about emotional flow and logical clarity. In change management, it's about making complex shifts feel navigable and motivating. A good change story:

- Ties logic and emotion together.
- Is repeated often, not just announced once.
- Evolves as the rollout progresses.

It's the job of leaders and enablement to make the purpose, process, and progress of a change clear. They must deliver that message consistently across formats, meetings, threads, 1:1s, and team huddles. When people know what's happening, and what isn't, they're less likely to feel caught off guard or left behind.

So, who drive's this communication and change? While you must have a change management plan, the executors of the plan are often the enablement team. Despite the growing presence in commercial teams, enablement is often boxed into training decks, new hire onboarding, and communications delivery. This makes them reactive and scattered, fire extinguishers to point at the "problem of the day". As someone who has worked in the field for almost two decades, it is a frustrating misunderstanding to fight through.

When done right, they are the bridge between strategy and execution and the glue that binds commercial teams like ops, strategy, product, sales, and customer success. They turn good ideas into real behavior. Unfortunately, we rarely give our enablement experts the room to be thoughtful and deliberate.

Their roles encompass training, coaching, resources, examples of what good and bad look like, practice and certification, champion-building, reinforcement, alignment with the other involved groups, and alignment to the final outcomes. If you aren't allowing your enablement teams to work this deeply and dedicated, you are wasting their expertise and losing productivity, wasting the talent of your commercial teams, and wasting the time and energy of your initiatives.

If we think of our change initiative as the journey, then enablement is the vehicle that gets you there.

Making Change Stick

It's good to remember that the first version of anything isn't going to be flawless. You will need to collect feedback, test, and adjust. Your initiative's launch is not the finish line. Wherever possible, you must involve all affected teams early. This way you gather input during planning, not just after the rollout.

Affected teams have an ability to see where initiatives will impact them. Sometimes it is in a defensive way, or a resistant way, but this is natural. Getting through these barriers earlier and with a champion will help the main rollout run much smoother.

This is why a pilot phase, when possible, is so important. Sometimes you need to more quickly and a pilot cannot be run the way we all want to. But getting a respected peer from each group to be part of the testing and rollout will build buy-in and allow the behavior to be modeled, not just told.

A top-down mandate is usually seen as a decision made in the ivory tower of leadership, not considering what the troops on the ground will face. Taking time to co-create and help shape the change will drive ownership and willingness. It is the difference between people feeling something was *done to* them and feeling that they were a *part of* something.

It is taking the idea that needs to become a reality and putting it into the context of real work. Commercial teams need to see this in order to make these changes. New tools and systems, or processes and methodologies, need to be clearly attached to expectations. Tied to the way things work now, how they need to work in the future, and how these updates enhance their lives and the lives of their customers.

This involves creating just-in-time resources that are also in-context and easy to access. Ensuring that coaching conversations and 1:1s include these initiatives, and not just focused on tactical discussions. For sales and customer success teams, we tend to focus almost exclusively on deal progression facts, but not on the skills needed to progress them. The learning curve flattens much faster when teams feel supported and learning is continuous.

Doing this helps us to get quick wins early.

One of the things that I like to build into programs are "quick wins". These are small things that happen early but build big momentum. Quick wins build credibility with the teams and help them see what is possible if they implement this change. Always look for ways to identify these small successes, publicize them, and celebrate them. Involve the individuals and teams who model the desired behaviors to show that the change is real and that it is working. As you do this, others will see that it is worth the effort, and they will be more likely to do it as well.

But finding these wins can take time and energy. We live in a world that either wants to be static, or to change so fast that anything done yesterday is too old. We need to be careful not to change for the sake of change but also need to realize that we are not stationery. And neither is the rollout of your initiatives.

While we involve the right people in the creation and rollout, we must also provide feedback loops once launched. You should collect feedback via surveys and open forums, and even during team meetings. Managers and leadership should observe the frontlines and gather information during coaching sessions on what is and isn't working. This helps to surface obstacles early on before they turn into cynicism. It also shows that honest feedback leads to real adjustments.

The key is to not just collect feedback, but to act on it as well.

Even the best-implemented efforts need reinforcement. New behaviors will not solidify magically after a single announcement or even the first training. Enablement needs to be consistent in their rollout, emphasis, and support. Leaders must walk the talk by setting aside old tools, metrics, and processes in order to model the behavior they require from their teams.

Dripping enablement just-in-time to be useful will keep teams from forgetting the changes. Recognizing those who are doing it right and baking it all into the new workflows will also reinforce the change. Take the content and replace the old ways in onboarding, checklists, processes, and wherever else the change needs to take place. Empower your managers to course-correct gently and consistently as teams work to adopt the new habits.

We often assume we will rise to the occasion, but in reality, our old habits sneak back in quietly, even with the best of intentions. Often, rollouts don't fail loudly, but they do fade away unless it is actively sustained.

Chapter Wrap

Here's what kills good ideas: bad implementation.

It's not enough to send an email, host an office hour, roll out a slide deck, and hope for the best. Change takes reinforcement, feedback loops, and a whole lot of clarity.

Try this with your team:

- **Review:** What's one change we rolled out that didn't stick? Why?
- **Equip:** Are managers prepared to model and coach the behavior we need?
- **Support:** What does real support look like beyond launch day?

Now that we've laid the groundwork for thoughtful change it's time to make it stick. Let's dig into how systems scale because they are built with sustainability in mind.

THE ENABLEMENT ECOSYSTEM

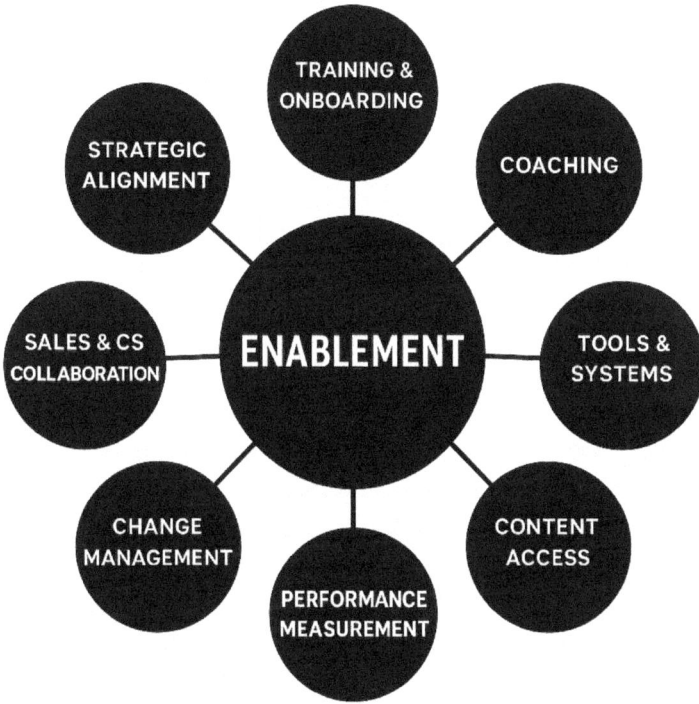

The Enablement Ecosystem — *High-impact enablement connects teams, tools, training, and outcomes. It's not an isolated function — it's embedded infrastructure.*

9

Scaling and Sustaining Productivity Systems

S*mall wins don't scale by accident. To grow productivity across a company, you need systems that flex without fracturing. This chapter is about scaling your strategy without sacrificing clarity, culture, or your team's capacity.*

> *"You do not rise to the level of your goals. You fall to the level of your systems."*
> —**James Clear**

As companies grow, so does complexity. Scaling often breaks many productivity initiatives because of this. There are more people and more processes, more communication channels and more levels of management, more tools and more systems, and more priorities that are competing with each other.

The systems we put in place need constant and active stewardship so that this complexity does not dilute clarity or create friction. And since we are changing our mindset from focusing on more outputs, to increasing our capacity to produce desired outcomes, this complexity actually undermines our capacity.

So how do we build a system designed to scale without sacrificing focus, alignment, or culture?

Growing companies often face the same predictable traps. Without intentional correction, these traps turn promising growth into a creeping dysfunction.

Issue	Description
Bloat	New roles, layers of management, and processes are added without simplifying or sunsetting old ones.
Tool Sprawl	Departments buy different platforms for the same problems, creating silos, duplicated effort, and integration nightmares.
Lost Clarity	Teams lose sight of the true strategic priorities as communication complexity rises.
Broken Communication Loops	As layers increase, feedback from the front lines gets muffled — and leadership decisions drift further from reality.

When designing a process or system to scale, we need to avoid trying to preserve rigid systems. This is not scaling. These rigid systems will crack and crumble under pressure.

Consider the construction of a high-rise building. It is not rigid; it needs to sway and move, shrink and expand. However, it does this with the boundaries built in already. High-rise buildings are designed to be flexible and resilient, allowing them to withstand various forces such as wind, earthquakes, and temperature changes. This flexibility is crucial for maintaining their structural integrity.

A scalable system must also have built-in boundaries that allow for flexibility and growth. Rigid systems, like a brittle building, will fail under pressure. In contrast, adaptable systems can thrive and evolve, just as a well-designed high-rise building can sway and move without collapsing.

The sway and flexibility you build into most systems are for people to act within a boundary but with the skills and knowledge necessary to complete the work. You need to preserve clarity, alignment, and adaptability. High-performing organizations ensure that they are focused on outcomes not just outputs.

They prioritize alignment over uniformity. Not every team has, or needs, identical processes. Teams do, however, need to understand and align on the same outcomes. Agreement on what success is and what good looks like are important. But so is understanding what aspects are non-negotiable. Where can a team flex, sure—but where must teams remain consistent.

Simplification before addition is another key principle. We often think that a new system, role, policy, or process will fix what is going wrong or enhance what is going right. But we need to ask first if this addition will allow us to eliminate anything redundant or unnecessary. It is a chance to take stock and simplify, eliminating the parts that have outlived their purpose.

Enablement isn't just for commercial reps and new hires, and it isn't just for launches and certifications. It is for everyone, and it is ongoing. As complexity increases, enablement is there to constantly re-orient teams, managers, and executives. This continuous enablement across tools, strategies, expectations, and ways of working keeps alignment tight and performance high while scaling.

I've been hammering home enablement these past few chapters. And for good reason, since it is the connective tissue of scalable systems. But enablement alone isn't enough. To sustain performance as you grow, you need to actively build capacity.

Building Capacity at Scale

If you want to move your team from output focus to building capacity to drive outcome, you need to start by clarifying what matters most. Every team needs to know exactly what they are striving for. What is their purpose and why are they doing the work that they do? This gives everyone something to drive toward.

And it will help them prioritize what they spend their time on, where they look for optimizations, and how to create real value. I've used the term "value" a few times already, and I will use it more throughout the book. Let me take a moment to clarify that value here is not defined how most leaders would, where it is providing bottom-line profits to the shareholders. In this book, value means producing something meaningful for the business, for customers, and for employees.

For a CSM, it might be reducing churn through a trust-based renewal. For a sales leader, it's surfacing the right deals and building scalable pipeline. For marketing, it's aligning content with what actually moves a deal forward. Value isn't just what shows up on the balance sheet — it's what creates traction, trust, and transformation.

When we are able to do this, and define value in this manner, we naturally look for ways to trim, automate, or deprioritize everything else. We want to spend our time on things that matter. The problem, though, is that in our haste we deprioritize things that matter but to the process but are too complicated. Think about how many conversations you've had with sales teams about updating the CRM. This stuff matters, but it feels tedious, and is often also found in other systems—so they deprioritize it since the information is still out there somewhere.

If leadership and departments are clear on what matters, they spend their time fixing processes and systems to match these priorities. Too often, processes and tool stacks complicate and convolute the situation. Teams have two or three locations to enter their information or find their tasks. The interoperability that is promised between systems turns out to be tricky or still on the roadmap, meaning that the sharing between tools isn't happening.

Teams then focus their time in the tools that matter most to them, rather than what matters most to the leadership. Dashboards stop updating with the best data, and activity metrics are the fallback again. We will talk more about tools in a future chapter, but this is a common issue I've seen in many organizations, where the rush to get the "best tools" creates fatigue and complexity that wears down even the best teams.

Besides making it easier to enter or access information, it is important to coach leadership and teams on capacity and outcomes. Instead of activity numbers, focus on quality and results. Measure your progress towards strategic goals. Give people at all levels of the organization access to training, learning, guidance, and focused time.

Beyond the business results, the shift here is human-focused. Think back to your professional, or even student careers. Have you ever experienced burn-out? Was it because you worked hard? Likely not. Most people enjoy hard work, especially when it is something that they believe in or find value in.

Most people burn out because they overwork on things that don't matter. Constantly running in circles, focused on the wrong things. You were too focused on school or work. You were spending time working on projects that never went anywhere. You were constantly tracked on tasks and asked to increase them, while ignoring the actions that created impact.

Capacity both operational and emotional. When people work toward outcomes that matter, they feel energized, not depleted. Clarity fuels motivation. Progress drives momentum. Outcome-focused teams are both more effective and more resilient. When teams spin their wheels without seeing progress or meaning in their work, exhaustion is inevitable.

When teams are focused on producing valuable outcomes at capacity they perform better. They also feel better, keep talent longer, and innovate more effectively. The environment created is collaborative and healthy, and the work is worth it.

Moving beyond output obsession is the first step, but it certainly is not the last one. We will all try and fail and try again as we fight to overcome decades, even centuries, of deeply ingrained perceptions of productivity.

Why a System

As a company is starting out, it is common to rely on heroics to grow the customer base and expand operations. As the company grows, this leads to too many different ways of doing things—even on the same teams. Heroism can work when you are trying to salvage a quarter or impress investors, but it is not going to scale or last. That is why your organization needs a system early.

Systems are how we capture institutional knowledge. We fill out playbooks, learning libraries, FAQs, and guides. We create new hire onboarding and ongoing enablement from this knowledge. We also build repeatable processes where possible, which include identifying the skills and characteristics necessary for success and implementing them into the coaching programs.

Creating systems helps identify clear decision-making frameworks. This allows teams to know who owns what, and people to know when or if they need to reach out to others. It also reduces the risk of tool sprawl and tool fatigue we talked about earlier.

A good system empowers teams while connecting to core goals. Allowing people to ramp faster, perform better, and contribute meaningfully. It is a balance of autonomy and alignment that guides outcome without requiring massive amounts of strength and will. The system enhances the work of the people.

As an organization grows, focus becomes more critical but also gets harder. To combat this, we need to protect clarity at scale.

Strategy	Details
Simplify strategic plans	Stick to a few true priorities at any one time
Create cascading goals	Ensure team and individual goals clearly link to company-level outcomes
Communicate priorities relentlessly	Not once a year. Constantly. Through all-hands, team meetings, 1:1s, and informal channels
Say no	Protect capacity by turning down projects, tools, or initiatives that don't align

Protecting Culture During Growth

If the vibes are "off", you've got a problem. But culture is more than a vibe. It is shared beliefs, behavior, and ways of working (WOW). Without intentional stewardship, culture cracks during scaling. As organizations grow, it becomes increasingly important to protect and nurture the culture that has been built.

First, you must codify core values and behaviors by identifying real, observable actions that you expect from everyone in the organization. Avoid buzzwords and fleeting principles and focus on tangible behaviors that reflect the company's values. These core values should be ingrained in every aspect of the organization, from hiring practices to daily interactions internally and externally.

Hiring and promoting with cultural alignment in mind is crucial. While most jobs and skills can be taught, misaligned values can compound over time and create significant issues. When evaluating new hires or candidates for promotion, consider how they match the company's values, as well as their performance. This ensures that the culture remains consistent and strong.

Publicly recognize individuals who embody the values and behaviors that the company wants to protect as it grows. This not only reinforces the importance of these values but also encourages others to follow suit. Recognition can take many forms, from awards and shout-outs in your regular meetings or newsletters to something more formal.

Your culture must be integrated into your systems. Embed the company's values into onboarding processes, goal setting, performance reviews, strategy, and daily rituals. This ensures that new employees understand and embrace the culture from day one, and that existing employees are continually reminded of its importance. Scaling culture isn't about simply enforcing rules but rather amplifying the best parts of your organization intentionally and visibly.

As organizations grow, leadership must evolve. Small team leadership often involves close relationships, direct coaching, and personal involvement in day-to-day work. However, at scale, leadership must shift toward setting vision and direction, building and reinforcing systems, developing other leaders, and focusing on strategic levers rather than tactical fire drills.

Micromanagement doesn't scale. And neither do heroics. But a great system will.

One of the key aspects of effective leadership is setting a clear vision and direction for the organization. This involves communicating the company's goals and objectives clearly and consistently and ensuring that everyone understands their role in achieving them. Building and reinforcing systems is also crucial. Leadership does this by creating processes and structures that support goals and values and ensuring that they are consistently applied across all teams.

Developing other leaders is another important aspect of leadership at scale. This involves identifying and nurturing potential leaders within the organization and providing them with the tools and support they need to succeed. By developing a strong leadership pipeline, organizations can ensure that they have the talent and expertise needed to navigate periods of growth and change.

Focusing on strategic leverage points rather than tactical fire drills is essential. By identifying the key areas where the organization can have the greatest impact and focusing resources and efforts on these areas. And by prioritizing strategic initiatives, leaders can ensure that the organization is moving in the right direction and achieving its goals.

Protecting culture during growth and evolving leadership at scale are vital for the long-term success of any organization. By codifying core values, hiring for cultural alignment, celebrating culture-carriers, integrating culture into systems, and shifting leadership focus, organizations can ensure that they remain strong, vibrant, and successful as they grow.

Cultivating a Productivity-Driven Culture

Effective leaders understand that how they approach their teams has a huge influence on their overall performance. Collaboration and open communication give teams the space they need to express their ideas without fear and share best practices.

I have worked with many startups on their upward trajectory, and with companies that were going through tough times and needed to rethink what their focus was. The difference between a healthy organization and an unhealthy one was evident during the first meetings I attended. If teams were quiet and not answering questions or giving ideas, they had already checked out. The damage was done. They had decided that it was not safe to be honest.

These teams were usually working unclear expectations, ambiguous goals, and shifting priorities. And even though they were on the front lines, if they raised honest questions they were labeled as troublemakers or squeaky wheels. While it is common to have people that are just upset no matter what the decision is, it is very rare that most people will be—unless they have been through the ringer already.

That's why it is so important to make sure that any changes you are implementing do not disrupt existing workflows. Unless, of course, that is the goal. If your workflows are broken, they should be disrupted. But you need to be clear with the affected teams on why this is a necessary thing. Be transparent and collaborative with regular check-ins.

Ultimately, to bring your teams on board with productivity and capacity improvement, you need to do more than just add tools and automate processes. Engage your teams with an atmosphere where you celebrate successes and recognize contributions. As your teams work together on their goals, and are rewarded for their insight and input, they will welcome the shift and drive their own productivity and growth.

Chapter Wrap

Scaling is when things get real because what works for 5 people might break with 50. But the answer isn't always more process, more controls, or more tools. It's clarity and designing for flexibility and accountability.

Try this with your team:

- **Evaluate:** What's starting to break or slow us down as we grow?
- **Define:** Where do we need consistency vs. where can teams flex?
- **Simplify:** What's one process we can streamline today?

We've come a long way on this journey from output to capacity and from vanity metrics to real clarity. Now let's wrap it up with one final lens: how to lead through all of this without burning your people out.

10

Building Sustainable, Human-First Productivity

B urnout isn't a badge of honor. *Sustainable productivity is built on clarity, resilience, and respect for human limits. In this final chapter, we'll explore how to lead and build in a way that performs today and endures tomorrow.*

> *"Working hard for something we do not care about is called stress; working hard for something we love is called passion."*
> —**Simon Sinek**

I have had the privilege of being a coach for my son's baseball teams for a few years. I did not grow up playing baseball, so I never expected to be in this position. However, I can see principles of productivity in how the players play, and it makes sense to use them in certain ways. If we are talking about speed, the first thing in baseball that usually comes up is pitching. How fast does someone throw the ball? But the thing is, it doesn't matter how fast they throw it if they can't get it over the plate. A wild pitch to the backstop will score an opposing run, even if it is thrown fast.

In business, speed matters. I argued earlier that quickness is more important than speed, yet we prioritize speed over almost everything else today. But when we strip away all the metrics, tools, and methodologies, productivity has never really been about speed because speed by itself doesn't take us where we want to go. We need a destination and a clear map to get there. Productivity is about the outcome.

We build capacity, align efforts to outcomes, measure the impact, and create systems that elevate potential. What we are trying to do with this book is to move beyond hustle and vanity metrics and short-term velocity. These things can have a place but are not the focus. The future belongs to organizations that understand it isn't always about how much you can do, but how much you can achieve.

Throughout this book, one principle has surfaced repeatedly: Capacity is the true engine of sustainable productivity. It is the cornerstone of achieving long-term success and avoiding the pitfalls that come with mere output. Output without strategy leads to noise. Output without enablement leads to burnout. Output without outcomes leads to wasted potential.

Capacity, however, is different. It is about focused attention, high-leverage effort, strategic clarity, emotional and cognitive resilience, and systems that protect and expand human potential. When you build capacity, small teams do great things, individuals grow into high-impact contributors, and organizations scale intelligently instead of chaotically.

Capacity isn't about working more; but rather enabling more with the time, energy, and skills you have.

Systems and Sustainable Cultures

Heroic efforts are seductive. We love stories of the late-night project saves, the last-minute wins, the all-hands-on-deck scrambles. But heroics don't scale. Heroics are not sustainable. Real, lasting productivity is built on systems that make the right action the easy action. These systems remove friction instead of celebrating struggle and protect energy instead of draining it.

While a heroic effort and last-minute save is a great story, they create a culture where the underlying issues that necessitate these heroics are never addressed. Systems, on the other hand, create a framework where the right actions are the easiest to take. They remove obstacles and streamline processes, making it easier for individuals and teams to perform at their best. By reducing the need for constant firefighting and allowing people to focus on high-leverage activities that drive real results, systems create massive impact on our teams.

Hustle culture told us: work harder, work longer, sleep when you're dead. It celebrated exhaustion as a badge of honor. But leaders focused on true productivity know that sustainable cultures outperform hustle cultures every time. Teams that are healthy, focused, and supported innovate, adapt, and grow. When we reward strategic work over visible busyness we build loyalty, trust, and long-term results. Leaders who model sustainable behaviors, not burnout heroics, create organizations that last.

Hustle culture should be a relic of the past. It glorifies overwork and burnout, leading to short-term gains but long-term damage. It is entirely focused on the "now" and causes misalignment of priorities where speed is celebrated at the expense of quickness.

"Fail fast, fix fast" just leads to a lot of wasted effort in the constant building and fixing of programs and processes. Quickness focuses on moving with lightness, unencumbered by the burdensome. It shows trust in your teams to move quickly but shows fear when always moving fast.

Sustainable cultures understand that healthy, focused, and supported teams are more innovative, adaptable, and resilient. These cultures reward strategic work over visible busyness, building loyalty and trust among employees. Leaders who model sustainable behaviors set the tone for the entire organization, creating a culture that values long-term success over short-term heroics.

Empowering Humans with Technology

AI and automation are powerful and inevitable. They are reshaping what work looks like at every level. But the goal shouldn't be to simply replace humans. Although, let's be honest, there are jobs that will be highly automated and others that will disappear due to emerging technology. The goal instead should be to free our teams to focus where they are irreplaceable: judgment, empathy, creativity, strategic thinking, and relationship-building. The organizations that win will not be the ones with the most bots. They'll be the ones that pair human insight and AI efficiency to build capacity.

We talked about it earlier, the fear that AI and automation will replace human jobs is widespread, but it misses the point. These technologies are tools that can enhance human capabilities, not replace them. By automating routine tasks, AI augments your teams' abilities and allows them more time to focus on what they do best. Teams will build capacity by leveraging the strengths of both humans and machines, creating a more efficient and effective workforce.

To do this effectively, organizations need to adopt a strategic approach by identifying the areas where technology can have the most significant impact and integrating it into existing workflows. It also means providing training and support to ensure that individuals can use these tools effectively and efficiently.

Employee Well-being and Productivity

Employee well-being is increasingly recognized as a vital component of organizational productivity, but too often ends up as a checkbox about office perks (remember the StartupCo example in Chapter 3).

Teams that feel safe, clear, and supported are able to focus better, adapt faster, and deliver more consistent outcomes. Strategic well-being is a productivity lever, not simply an employee perk. Initiatives such as flexible working hours, mental health resources, and wellness programs can create an environment where employees feel valued and motivated, but these things alone do not create well-being. They need to also know their work adds value.

The relationship between employee well-being and productivity is supported by studies highlighting the correlation between job satisfaction and performance metrics. Employees who experience a positive work environment are less likely to suffer from burnout and stress-related issues. Automation plays a key role in employee well-being by streamlining repetitive tasks and freeing up valuable time for more meaningful work. The integration of automation into processes can allow teams to focus on more strategic initiatives where they are able to utilize and grow their skills.

As we talk about increasing capacity, we need to remember that capacity planning is critical. Leaders need to understand the available resources and what their teams are currently working in order to allocate work effectively. This type of planning helps prevent overloading their teams and keeps focus on high-value goals.

In this new era of work, leadership demands clarity over complexity, capacity-building over task-pushing, enablement over micromanagement, and adaptability over rigidity. Leaders must become stewards of systems, culture, and capacity, instead of just managers of tasks. The best leaders will measure their success not by how much noise their teams create, but by how much meaningful, lasting impact they enable.

They understand that their role is to empower their teams, not micromanage them.

Success is often measured by metrics that don't tell the whole story. Hours logged, dashboards lit up, and reports generated are all indicators of activity, but they don't necessarily reflect real progress. The true mark of success is how clearly a team understands what matters, how consistently they align their efforts with real outcomes, how effectively they grow capacity without burning people out, and how resiliently they adapt to changing circumstances. True success is measured by sustained impact, meaningful progress, and desired outcomes. That kind of clarity doesn't happen by accident. As we saw in Chapter 8, it requires reinforcement, thoughtful enablement, and leadership that supports adoption.

Implementing the New Productivity Model

We've talked about systems a few times, but we haven't really dug into developing a customized productivity framework. This framework serves as a tailored approach that aligns with the unique objectives, culture, and workflows of a specific team or organization. The foundation is built in carefully assessing the capabilities and the gaps that need to be enhanced and addressed.

The first step is difficult and is the conducting of a thorough analysis of existing workflows. Team by team, and person by person, you need to map out each process in order to visualize how tasks are performed. Doing this helps you to identify bottlenecks and redundancies, but it also helps you clarify how teams, departments, and individuals work together. What dependencies do they have that haven't been codified?

Engaging team members in this analysis can provide valuable insights, as they often have firsthand knowledge of the challenges faced in their daily tasks. This collaboration gives a sense of ownership among team members and ensures that the framework is grounded in real-world experiences. But be careful, because if you are unclear as to why this is happening, it can lead to resistance and pushbacks as individuals assume they are being brought to task rather than cooperating to create clearer and better work experiences.

It is important to note that some people thrive on ambiguity and complexity, sitting in the shadows and avoiding the harsh light of accountability. While you shouldn't expect this to be a lot, it is more than likely that you will come across people who are not producing much and will resist this stage of the process.

Once the analysis is complete, the next stage is to establish clear goals. Goals could be anything from improving response times in customer service to increasing follow-up rates in sales teams. The main objective of this stage is to clearly align team goals to organizational objectives. While it makes sense when said aloud, it is often overlooked, and teams wind up making their own goals in a vacuum. The focus on alignment here leads to more motivated teams as they more easily see how what they do directly impacts larger organizational success.

When you are building this framework, be sure to incorporate automation in order to enhance capacity. We've talked about tools in Chapters 5 & 6 but be sure to choose solutions that streamline repetitive tasks, reduce the margin for error, and free up valuable time for team members to focus on higher-level, strategic activities. Be sure to provide the right training and support as well, so these tools and initiatives get off on the right foot, and everyone has what they need to perform their best.

And just like anything else you implement, it is important to continuously monitor and adjust the productivity framework. Hold regular feedback sessions and to help identify what is working well and what needs refinement. Clear and effective metrics should be established to track progress against the defined goals and objectives.

Goals provide direction and purpose.

Metrics serve as specific milestones that guide teams toward achieving broader aspirations.

Chapter Wrap

This is the shift. From busy to better. From doing more to doing what matters. From chasing productivity to designing for it.

You don't need to be a perfect leader. But you do need to be an intentional one.

Try this with your team:

- **Protect:** Carve out time to reflect. Are we just sprinting, or are we learning?
- **Assess:** What's energizing vs. what's draining? How do we respond?
- **Prioritize:** Is building capacity a leadership priority or just a team problem?

Busy vs. Better

Busy	Better
Chasing activity for activity's sake	Prioritizing for maximum impact
Measuring metrics that don't matter	Measuring outcomes that do
Rewarding motion	Building capacity
Manual and rigid	Automated and adaptive
Stuck in survival mode	Set up to succeed

Busy vs. Better — One is the default. The other is a choice. Use this lens when evaluating your systems, rituals, and metrics.

Afterword

If you've made it this far then something inside you already knew that the way we've been working isn't working.

You've probably felt it yourself. The creeping burnout, the constant flood of meetings, the nagging sense that even though your team is busy all the time... they're not really moving forward. Maybe you've seen talented people check out, systems get bloated, or tools that promised to help actually make things worse.

Or maybe it was just a gut feeling that has been nagging at you that what there has to be a better way.

So Where Do You Start?

You don't need a perfect plan that boils the ocean. You just need to pick one place where things feel stuck or overly complex. This is where you see motion, but no movement.

Throughout this book, we've returned to a set of foundational ideas that support a new way of thinking about productivity. Let's revisit them one last time:

- **Output vs. Outcome:** Real success is measured by the significance of the impact. Busy teams often hit their numbers. Better teams move the mission.

- **Capacity over Headcount:** Productivity starts with doing more with what you already have. When capacity is built intentionally, teams grow stronger, not just larger.
- **Strategic Streamlining:** Cutting isn't the enemy. Blind cutting is. Strategic streamlining is about protecting momentum by removing friction and realigning resources with purpose.
- **Tools that Amplify:** Technology should clarify, not complicate. The right tools reduce overhead, surface insight, and extend human capability. The wrong tools distract, confuse, and drain.
- **Metrics that Matter:** Easy-to-measure often becomes easy to overvalue. True productivity metrics track outcomes, not just effort. What you measure shapes what your team believes matters.
- **Change that Sticks:** Change is easy to talk about, hard to land. It takes intentional sequencing, communication, and follow-through to ensure shifts aren't just attempted but adopted.
- **Human-Centered Systems:** Organizations don't scale on process alone. They scale on people. And people scale when they are respected, enabled, and aligned with something bigger than themselves.

Every one of these ideas converges on a single truth: productivity is not about doing more things. It's about doing the right things, at the right time, with the right support.

The most effective leaders don't win by pushing harder. They win by creating the conditions for clarity to thrive. They balance culture with accountability and know that vague priorities create chaos and rigid systems create burnout. They know that sustainable productivity is where alignment meets autonomy.

You don't need to be perfect to start. You don't need to rebuild everything from scratch. But you do need to ask the question:

- "Are my teams clear on what matters, why it matters, and how their work contributes to it?"

If the answer isn't a confident yes, that's your cue for where to start. Pick one priority to realign or one workflow to clarify. Use what you already have and remove what doesn't serve. Go small to go fast, and once it works — scale it.

You don't need to fix everything. But you do need to create the conditions where better work becomes inevitable, and where progress is felt, not just measured. Where people thrive, and outcomes compound.

You've already taken the first step by questioning the old playbook. You've dared to imagine something better.

Now comes the courageous part: choosing better over busy. Every day.

So, what's your move?

About the Author

Mike Garber is an enablement and productivity leader with over 20 years of experience building systems that help teams scale without burning out. From early operational roles to leadership positions in enablement, sales, and strategy, he's spent two decades helping organizations move from reactive work to sustainable performance.

Known for his clarity-first approach and practical frameworks, Mike specializes in helping teams streamline complexity, unlock capacity, and align their systems to outcomes that matter. He holds a Master's degree in Management & Leadership and brings a grounded, human perspective to every team and challenge he supports.

Outside of work, Mike spends time with his wife and three kids playing games, exploring nature, shuttling between baseball and dance practices, and finding ways to build their love for history and science. He's also served as a youth advisor at his church for over a decade — a role that keeps him grounded, learning, and connected.

You can connect with me on:

- https://www.frombusytobetter.com
- https://x.com/hifimike11
- https://www.linkedin.com/in/wmikegarber
- https://www.tdsconsultingllc.com